When Theo Met Meta

by

Daniel Shaw Coleman

When Theo Met Meta

A History of the Coleman-Shaw
Families Of Valdosta, Georgia

by

Daniel Shaw Coleman

2014

ISBN: 978-0-9907009-3-7 (Hardcover)
First Hardcover Edition
The Lightwood History Collection: Book 8

Cover photograph of Theo, Meta, Dan and Wade Coleman, 1944

Cover and Interior Design by Josh Sheffield

Contents

Preface

During the preparation of our family history, I realized that one of the most striking aspects of our heritage is just how deep our Southern roots run. All of our ancestors arrived in the North American colonies prior to the Revolutionary War, and then, with one exception, they all settled in the Southeastern states prior to that war. The exception is Reuben Charles, who moved about 1792 with his parents from Pennsylvania to South Carolina. Also surprising is that all of these families had settled in either South Georgia or North Florida prior to the Civil War. We are also a pretty homogeneous family group in that we are all descendants of emigrants from the British Isles: England, Wales, Scotland and Ireland. While I was unable to determine the place of overseas origin of every emigrant ancestor, I feel fairly certain, based on their names and other information, that this statement applies to all of them.

I also found that all our ancestors were men of the soil. They were farmers, or if they did not practice farming as their main source of income, as in the case of the Charles family, they did have farming interests. They were not professional men or soldiers or government workers or miners or engaged in any other such occupation. We did have one merchant family, one clergyman *cum* farmer and one railroad man prior to the twentieth century. Of course some of our ancestors labored in the lumber or turpentine industry, but tree farming or harvesting was a form of farming as well. Some of our farmer ancestors were large plantation owners, others yeomen farmers who worked the land by themselves, with the help of their own large families.

The number of children in our farm families in the nineteenth century is truly astonishing. Of the forty families profiled here, nineteen consisted of families with eight or more children, of which two had sixteen. But since their parents were mostly farmers, children were farm hands, not just mouths to feed and bodies to clothe. Our ancestors lived in the countryside, usually on their farms, or if not, in the small nearby cities. Think of Cobbtown with 338 inhabitants in 1990, Eastman with 5,153, Lake City with 10,005, and Valdosta, the largest at 39,806 that year. And those places were much, much smaller during the 1800s where most of our ancestors noted here lived. No Atlanta or Savannah or Macon for them.

As stated, our ancestors were not professional soldiers but when war forced itself on them, they fought. The list of our Revolutionary War ancestors who fought against the British so far number nine: John Tillman, John Everett, Henry Holland, William Hendley, Stewart Hamilton, Thomas Horne (who died while serving), David Horton, Richard Horne and George Carter. No Tory soldiers were found. All but John Everett and Richard Horne have been documented as Revolutionary War soldiers and so designated by the DAR or the SAR as Patriots. Also, Elizabeth Horne has been designated a DAR Patriot as a result of supplying provisions to the Continental Line. Only one was an officer, John Tillman, while the rest were enlisted men, again proof that they were only wartime soldiers.

The same is true with respect to the Civil War. Irvin Brown Hamilton (who died while serving), Larkin Hargrove, William Shaw and Reuben Charles all fulfilled the commitment to defend their homes. Several others served in state militias but did not engage in the fighting. They all served the Confederacy although a few had siblings who were with the Union.

Were our ancestors educated men? No, not in today's meaning. I believe that most could read the Bible, at the very least, and many could write—well and not so well—however, there was not much need for a farmer to have the ability to write. Nor were they very good at it even when the need arose, as some of the letters and extracts here show. Most had a modicum of education, either from a family tutor or a one room school for a few months a year. Surely some were illiterate. I have seen documents in which a few of our ancestors' legal signature consisted of an "X." It wasn't until the second quarter of the twentieth century that the first college graduates emerged, our parents, Theo and Meta.

Yet they also used what talents and abilities they had to serve their communities. Many served as justice of the peace, judge of an inferior court, petit and/or grand juror, state legislator, county commissioner and so on. They also served on committees or commissions as needed. They were expected to fulfill those civic responsibilities, which they did.

Like all families we have our warts. Slavery was a common and an accepted practice in the South and for large farmers it was the only way to operate a farm. We know today that it should not have been legal, as it was, nor in any way acceptable. Yet Southerners paid a big price trying to preserve their way of life, the price being the lives of many of their sons, as we see here. But we are not here to judge them, even though we might deeply regret their actions. Our ancestors also had their passions, as we all do, and you will read about the times when their passions overruled their good sense. But let's leave them alone. Isn't there something in the Bible about casting stones?

Anyway, read for yourselves all about your ancestors. I hope you will have a pleasurable experience and, maybe, you might learn a little bit more about yourself.

The reader will please note that my mother's first name, Meta, is pronounced *Mee' tuh*, as in the word meet.

Introduction

This is a book of history, and, like all such books, its purpose is to tell a story of a time and a place and the people who were there. But in presenting this history I have used a genealogy format, one that traces our family history tree or chart as far back as six generations, depending on the family tree being drawn. In this way I am able to identify and write about our parents, our four grandparents, our eight great grandparents and our sixteen great-great grandparents, all of whom passed on their genes to us. In most cases I can go back at least one more generation and in a couple of cases, even a couple of generations further, but no more. The Revolutionary War is the general starting point for each family tree because information on most of the lineages discussed here is very sparse prior to that period. But that level of information is enough to give a pretty good idea of who our ancestors were and what our family is all about.

The purpose of this book is to help me and, I hope, others in our family who one day will read this book, to have a much better idea of the people whose blood they carry in their veins and how they lived and died. To me, it is fascinating to read about them, how they carried out their daily tasks, how they coped with adversity, what they were involved in, and how the times are so different than times today. Some lived quiet lives, others very active and interesting lives. Some lived in exciting times, others in times of peace and prosperity, even boring. But all are worth knowing about if you want to understand your own make up.

I decided to start the book by developing a family tree for each of our four grandparents—Coleman, Hargrove, Shaw and Charles—giving each of them a chapter with a geographical name. In each of the four chapters there are four lineages, for a total of sixteen, with each lineage having one to four families. At the beginning of each lineage I try to give a brief history of its origins, some of which are quite extensive, even going back to an emigrant ancestor to the New World or even earlier; others are fairly brief as little was found prior to the identification of the first ancestor noted in the chapter.

Let me give an example. The Pine Barrens family tree consists of the Coleman, Tillman, Everett, and Holland lineages all of which are branches of a single family tree. The Coleman lineage, one of the four branches, includes four descending Coleman families or generations: starting with Wade W., then followed by Jeremiah, Daniel Wade and Daniel Ernest, the last in that lineage. The same layout is shown for the other three family lineages. Altogether, exactly forty families are identified and discussed. The sequence is chapter or family tree, then lineage, then family. The fifth chapter brings together the four family trees to create a final tree of only one family, that of our parents, Theo Wade Coleman and Meta (pronounced "Meeta") Aubrey Shaw and their five sons.

I have tried to use as few abbreviations as possible. But some are necessary: "b"= born; "d"= died; "m"= married; and "unk"= unknown, are commonly used in the lists of each family's children. I have also abbreviated the months in that part. In the list of their children, the child in **bold lettering** is our direct ancestor. I have also placed a separate family tree on the second page of each of the first four chapters so that the reader can have a quick snapshot of the family to be covered in that particular chapter. The index will help the readers to locate all of their relevant ancestors

I started gathering information for this book in late 1997 after coming across a number of interesting documents in my mother's effects. This piqued my interest in our family history, and after spending years of research and preparing many drafts, mostly while living in the Washington, D. C., area, I finally completed this book just this year. While I had access to some very extensive state and federal archives and libraries in Washington and elsewhere, I also had help from a number of genealogists, most of whom are my aunts, cousins—distant and otherwise—many of whom I would never have met had I not become interested in our family's history. Let me mention a few: Dorothy Hargrove Stoeger, Corinne Coleman, Carlton Wood, Jerry Coleman, Stephen Whigham, David Crews, Milton Weeks, Virginia Shaw Girardin and David Girardin. I still stay in touch with some of them; others have died. And I would be remiss if I did not mention advice from Bo Williams, the finest genealogist I have ever known.

I have used DNA results to some effect, as in the case in which I was able to learn that Andrew Jackson Hargrove's unknown father was really a Hargrove and not so good when I tried to learn the name of Wade W. Coleman's father, which I did not. Maybe in the future enough men will undergo testing so that we will learn more, assuming also that additional research is undertaken. Anyone wishing to see more on Wade W. Coleman's descendants can go to *www.colemandna.com/genealogy*, the family tree number being 31738. In this way you can trace a great number of Wade W. Coleman's descendants. Or call me.

Writing about DNA reminded me that I have been asked where we came from, that is, information about our deep family origins. There are some hints. I had my DNA tested by Family Tree DNA and discovered that our Colemans have a J2 Haplotype, a haplotype being the terminology used to identify the different classifications of men who have a common ancestry. Men identified as J2 are thought to have originated in the Middle East between 15,000 and 22,000 years ago and who moved westward into Western Europe about 8,000 BC. The largest concentrations of J2s today are in the Northeast Caucasus region and in Central Anatolia, with the latter having one of the highest J2 concentrations at 30 percent. This is probably why my brother Wade and I, on different visits to Turkey, enjoyed ourselves so much in that country; we have a lot of relatives there.

I am sure I have made some mistakes, but I assure the reader that they were not intentional; instead they are the results of an untrained genealogist and historian at work. I am also sure that once this book is bound and distributed, I will come across another piece of information that I would have included had it come to my attention earlier. Such is life. But, also, as a result of this book's publication, perhaps someone will be able to take it and discover something new that sheds more light on our family and thereby adds it to our store of family knowledge. That is the hope of all genealogists, and certainly mine, too.

Before I leave this introduction, I would like to thank several people who provided me with much needed assistance in completing this book. First is my proof reader, Willa Valencia, who prevented me from embarrassing myself. Next is Stephen Whigham, my cousin from Eastman, who took the book from me, formatted it, and then had it printed. Finally, to my wife Carolyn, who showed so much patience with me over the last few months, when I was feverishly trying to finish up a multi-year, off-and-on project. But, after all, it was on my bucket list, and she recognized that fact. Thank you, Carolyn.

Chapter 1

The Pine Barrens
The Coleman Family

Family Tree for
Daniel Ernest Coleman: Pine Barrens
4 Generations

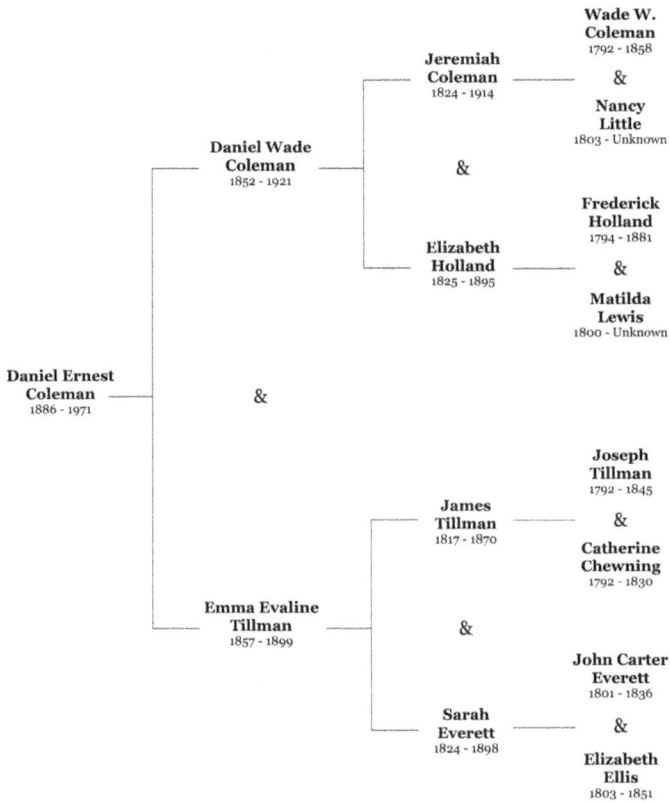

Wade W. Coleman
1792 - 1858

Jeremiah Coleman
1824 - 1914

&

Nancy Little
1803 - Unknown

Daniel Wade Coleman
1852 - 1921

&

Frederick Holland
1794 - 1881

Elizabeth Holland
1825 - 1895

&

Matilda Lewis
1800 - Unknown

Daniel Ernest Coleman
1886 - 1971

&

Joseph Tillman
1792 - 1845

James Tillman
1817 - 1870

&

Catherine Chewning
1792 - 1830

Emma Evaline Tillman
1857 - 1899

&

John Carter Everett
1801 - 1836

Sarah Everett
1824 - 1898

&

Elizabeth Ellis
1803 - 1851

Chapter 1

The Pine Barrens
The Coleman Family

The Pine Barrens family tree consists of those surname families who settled in and around that part of Georgia to the west of Savannah and north of the Altamaha River, which had opened up about twenty years after the Revolutionary War ended. This huge tract of forested land was originally designed as Washington County, but, over the years, more than fifteen counties have been carved out of it, with Tattnall County being only one, albeit the most important county for the Colemans and associated families. All four families that comprise this family tree have strong roots in the Pine Barrens area. The family lineages so discussed in this chapter are, naturally, the Colemans, but also the Hollands, Tillmans and Everetts. The family tree at the beginning of this chapter gives a succinct and graphic picture of this lineage.

The Coleman Lineage

The first authenticated Coleman in this line is Wade W. Coleman. While we do not know who his parents were, DNA records indicate a very close family relationship with a Moses Coleman—father, uncle, cousin?—who moved to Georgia shortly after the Revolutionary War, first settling in Washington County where he received a headright land grant in 1784. He then lived near Pendleton Creek, not far from Wade W. Coleman's home place. Researchers have found that Moses is descended from some Colemans who settled in Edgecombe County, North Carolina, after having left Virginia.

Robert Coleman of Nansemond County, Virginia, on the North Carolina border, had six sons, one being Moses (#1) and another Theophilus (#1). It is known that this Moses Coleman (#1), born 1740-1750, moved to Edgecombe County, North Carolina, where he sired three sons, one of whom was also named Moses (#2). Moses (#2), in turn, moved to Columbus County, North Carolina. It is highly likely that the Moses Coleman of Tattnall County is related to those Moses Colemans and, if true, then we could possibly trace our lineage back to Robert Coleman of Virginia. There is also a Theophilus (#2) Coleman who settled in Washington County about the same time as Moses Coleman and who died in Laurens County, Georgia, in 1816. Wade W. Coleman received a land grant in that same county. Is there any connection?

Until something new comes up, probably through DNA testing, we will not know.

Wade W. Coleman

Wade W. Coleman was born about 1792 somewhere in North Carolina and died in Tattnall County, Georgia, on March 12, 1858, age about sixty six. The name of his parents is still not known, nor is it known when he left North Carolina to move into Georgia. In 1821, Phillip Sapp, a Tattnall County justice of the peace, married Wade Coleman and Nancy Little of Bulloch County, Georgia. Her place of birth and parents are still debated although it is possible that an Archibald Little of Bulloch County is her father and a John Little of Tattnall is her brother. In the 1860 census she declares that her place of birth was Bulloch County, yet in the 1870 she says she was born in North Carolina, place unmentioned.

Wade's name first appears during the War of 1812, where a military record shows him as a private in Capt. John P. Blackmon's Company, 10th Battalion (Tattnall County), 2nd Brigade (Gen. Samuel Bryne's), 1st Division of Georgia Militia, serving a two months stint that began on January 10, 1814. His unit was stationed at Fort James on Milligan's Bluff at Payne's Landing on the Altamaha River, two miles north of Beard's Creek, and was posted there to protect the frontier against Indian attacks.

He is next mentioned in several state and county records as an acquirer of lands. In June 1818, Wade purchased 209 acres of pine land on the Ohoopee River in Tattnall County that had been sold at a sheriff's sale. On August 2, 1819, the State of Georgia granted him 100 acres on the west bank of the Ohoopee, adjoining his other property. That same year, Wade is shown as being eligible for one draw in the 1819 Georgia Land Lottery for Laurens County, which he may or may not have acted on. In the 1821 Georgia Land Lottery, he was awarded Lot 137 in Section 2 in Henry County which he most likely sold, given its distance from his home in Tattnall County.

On October 24, 1825, Wade surveyed two large adjacent tracts of land along the Ohoopee River in Tattnall County, one for 1,000 acres and the other for 600 acres, for which in 1831 he received headright grants from the State of Georgia. Then in 1837 the State awarded him another headright grant for a 973 acre tract which was located close to his other tracts. He also purchased another 200 acres in this same area from Littleberry Tillman. Obviously he was in the process of building up a substantial estate.

It is difficult to determine how much land Wade eventually accumulated. From tax records, deeds and his will it is likely that he owned at one time as much as 4,000 acres. Nearly all of this land was in the pine barrens belt which was considered inferior— and therefore much less valuable—than more fertile land appropriate for cotton and rice farming, the major crops in that area. It is known from his will that he had a sugar mill and boiler, so he must have grown some sugar cane along the river and creek beds.

By 1832 Wade established a toll ferry across the Ohoopee River. In 1833 he was appointed by the Tattnall County Inferior Court to a commission to "review the public utility of opening a road from the town of Reidsville to Wade Coleman's ferry on the Ohoopee and report to the Court." In June 1832 and again in June 1834 Wade was called to serve as a Tattnall County grand juror, a duty that reflected well in those days on his reputation in the community. In August 1839 he was named a commissioner of roads in Captain Tillman's Militia District. At some later date he was appointed to the Ohoopee River Fund, and, while the purpose of this fund is not known clearly, most likely it was to ensure that the river was kept open and free from obstructions so that logs— including his—could be floated to market.

In 1852 the county assessed Wade's property for tax purposes. He declared that he owned 3,113 acres of pine land at that time. On May 5, 1851, just before his tax declaration he had sold a 534 acre tract for $60 to Henry Anderson, the husband of his daughter, Mary. On February 12, 1853, he deeded 1,032 acres to his son Jeremiah for $100. In addition, he sold a 594 acre tract to his son Eli for $194 which was recorded after Eli's death by his brother, Jeremiah, the executor of latter's estate. All were at a price below the market rate. In this same tax record it shows that Wade declared the value of his estate at $3,219, of which the land value alone was $2,683. Clearly he was what was called "land poor."

Wade died in 1858 just ten days after making his will. Tattnall County Inferior Court records give his exact date of death as well as confirming his oldest son, Jeremiah, as his co-executor, along with James Tillman, his friend and neighbor. (Many years later, Jeremiah's son, Daniel Wade, would marry James Tillman's daughter, Emma Evaline.) Wade provided amply for his wife and children in his will. Wade's widow inherited 250 acres, their home and furnishings, as well all the livestock, farm equipment and tools. His son James received 491 acres while his daughter Margaret Ann got 400 acres. His retarded son, Wade Hampton, was left with 441 acres. His brother Jeremiah, having been named

Wade Hampton's guardian, was also left an additional 262 acres. His other children Eli and Mary only inherited $1 each since they had each been given a tract of land earlier when they married.

Little is known of Nancy Little Coleman, Wade's widow. She continued to live on the family property, probably for the rest of her life. Her unmarried daughter, Catherine, may have lived with her for some time, while her brother, Jeremiah, lived just down the road. She probably helped to rear the six grandchildren left orphans on the deaths of their fathers in the Civil War. In the 1870 census she is shown living at home with only a girl, Mary Cobb, sixteen. She did not appear in the 1880 census which indicates she must have died during the preceding ten year interval.

Wade and Nancy were buried on their property near the Ohoopee River. Present day relatives recall having once heard about some unmarked graves thereabouts but the exact location is still unknown. Most likely those are their graves of Wade and Nancy as well as of their son Wade Hampton.

Children of Wade W. Coleman and Nancy Little

1. Mary, b. Jun 5, 1822; d. Oct 2, 1892 in Tattnall County; m. Henry Anderson on Jan 16, 1845.

2. **James Jeremiah, b. Jan 5, 1824; d. Feb 17, 1914; m. Elizabeth Holland on Jan 3, 1850.**

3. Eli William, b. 1828; d. Nov 18, 1862; m. Martha Holland on Mar 14, 1862. Eli signed up with "B" Company ("Tattnall Rangers"), 61st Infantry Regiment of Georgia Volunteers and died of pneumonia in 1862 at a military hospital in Richmond, Virginia, where he was buried in an unmarked grave. Eli's widow never

6

remarried and remained on the land she inherited from her husband. She raised their five children alone, dying in 1908. Her sister and neighbor was Elizabeth Holland Coleman, Jeremiah's wife, who undoubtedly helped her to cope with her loss as well as to help rear her children.

4. Margaret, b. 1837; d. unk; m. Henry E. Gibbs on Feb 17, 1858. Henry served in Company "B", 61st Georgia Infantry Regiment. Jeremiah applied for a letter of administration for Henry Gibbs on January 21, 1868, meaning he was dead by then, whether during the Civil War or afterwards.

5. James L., b. 1839; d. Jun 10, 1862, m. Elvina Collins. James met his death at the Battle of Sessionville, South Carolina. This relatively obscure battle took place over a two-week period on James Island outside of Charleston, South Carolina. The eventual Confederate victory prevented the Union forces from taking this key port city. Actually he died at the skirmish called the Action at Grimball Farm. On June 10, 1862, six days before the major battle at Sessionville, his regiment was ordered to drive back an advanced Union line which was three miles from the main battle site. The Confederate troops charged dug-in positions but were stopped ten yards from reaching the Union lines and then driven back. Some sixty to seventy soldiers in James' regiment were killed or wounded in that action, a very high casualty rate. The Confederate soldiers killed that day, probably including James, were buried by the Union soldiers in unmarked graves. James was serving as a private with "G" Company ("Tattnall Invincibles"), 47th Infantry Regiment at the time. In 1866 his widow married William G. W. Hodges, and together they reared James's son, James, Jr.

6. Wade Hampton, b. 1843; d. Mar 27, 1862; never married. Wade's youngest child, Wade Hampton, was mentally retarded, being described in legal documents as an "idiot" or a "lunatic," which was a statement of fact in those politically incorrect days. He would also die in 1862 (like his two brothers) probably of an infirmity inherent in his condition. It is said that he was kind and gentle and could be trusted in most cases to be helpful to the family. One family legend is that once he was visiting at the home of one of his pregnant sisters whose husband was then serving in the Confederate Army. When labor pains came on she sent him to Jeremiah's home to get help from the women there. As Wade arrived dinner was being served so, being hungry, he sat down and ate. Only after he finished dinner did he remember to tell everyone why he came.

James Jeremiah Coleman

James Jeremiah Coleman, also called Jerry, was born in Bulloch County, not Tattnall County. It is thought that his mother may have been visiting some of her family there when his birth occurred in 1824. His parents were Wade W. and Nancy Little Coleman. On Jan 3, 1850, Jerry married Elizabeth Holland, the daughter of Frederick and Matilda Lewis Holland, who was born on March 13, 1825.

Jerry followed his father into the timber business and, appropriately enough, began to acquire land. In March of 1852 the state of Georgia granted him a 265 acre tract along Beard's Creek, adjacent to land that, apparently, he already owned. In 1853 his father sold him a piece of land consisting of 1,052 acres near the

Ohoopee River. Later in October 1855 he obtained a grant of another 654 acres abutting Beard's Creek which was next to land owned by William Coleman, probably a relative of his. In 1870 he purchased 248 acres from the estate of James Tillman, the future father-in-law of Jerry's son, Daniel. The ownership of his land is not clear, since it could, as well, have belonged to Jerry's sister, mother, or held by him in his role as guardian. In the 1860 property tax rolls, it showed that Jerry recorded ownership in the 441 acres belonging to his brother Wade; his mother's 250 acres; and his sister Catherine's 400 acres, in addition to his own land. In 1862 the county tax records show that Jerry valued his 2,013 acres at only $1,500, or about $.75/acre.

Jerry is first noted in Tattnall County records when the inferior court asked him and his father in February 1850 to "review a request to change the Old Dublin Road from Tillman's to Savannah." Their report was favorable, and apparently the route was changed. When his father died in 1858, he and James Tillman were executors of the estate. By the mid-1850s Jerry had begun to play a larger role in county affairs. He was both a grand juror and a petit juror in 1855 and, once again, a grand juror in 1860. From 1859 and throughout the Civil War he served as a Commissioner of Roads for the 351st Militia District, where all his land and home were located. In August 1860 Jerry was appointed a commissioner of the Ohoopee River Fund, filling a vacancy created by the death of his father earlier. Later he was appointed to "review the public utility of a road leading from Joseph Tillman's through Cobbtown and intersecting with Dublin Road above John Collins."

The outbreak of the Civil War had profound implications for Jerry and his extended family even though he did not serve in a military position. While he may have been somewhat overage at the beginning of the war to serve in a regular unit, by the time of Sherman's invasion of Georgia, he should have been inducted into a state militia unit at the very least. Yet this did not occur. One reason may have been that he had contracted typhoid fever in his youth causing him to suffer from periodic blackouts. This would have been grounds for a legitimate medical exemption. On the other hand, as will be seen below, he had major responsibilities on the home front rather than the battle front, which may have been grounds for a military exemption.

After the death of his two married brothers in 1862, Jerry's family responsibilities grew significantly. In addition to raising his own family of seven children, he was responsible for Eli's widow and her five children and for James' widow and her son. He was also responsible for looking out for his mother and unmarried sister. Fortunately Jerry's father had left all his children tracts of land giving Jerry additional resources to support all of his charges, but this only increased his work load. Among the various family members' property, there were thousands of acres of land to administer.

During the war period Jerry undertook a number of civic tasks to help soldiers' dependents living in Tattnall County. In March 1862 the inferior court appointed him as one of four commissioners in the 351st Militia District to assess the needs of the "families of the soldiers that are now in service, that are in indigent circumstances, and supply their necessities and make a report to the Court on the first Monday in June, 1862." In August 1863 he was appointed by the Court as an "overseer of invalids." That same year the county court named him a commissioner to "look after the families of indigent soldiers now in service and widows of soldiers and widowed mothers." Periodically the inferior court paid him funds which he distributed to needy families and widows of soldiers. He carried out these tasks until the end of the war.

With the war over Jerry focused on raising his extended family including Eli's orphans. Three of his sons, including Daniel until 1899, remained in Tattnall County all their lives, working their farms or applying their skills in the timber/turpentine industry. To some extent Jerry seems to have prospered after the war, not becoming rich, but probably better off than many others in the county who did not have the wherewithal to cope with the ordeals of Reconstruction. For one thing, he never owned any slaves so he did not suffer any property loss from such ownership. Also the destruction in the South created a big demand for building supplies, supplies that a man with large timber resources could handle. Lastly, the turpentine industry really began to take off in Georgia in the 1870's when Jerry was in his prime. These were products that he could and would supply. Evidence of this prosperity is that while he was able to provide only basic sporadic home schooling for most of his children, later on he was able to educate his youngest son, Jeremiah, Jr., at a real school.

Since Jerry lived until 1914 some stories about him are still around and have been retold by his descendants. One story tells of Jeremiah guiding a raft of logs down the river to Darien when he was confronted by another raft stuck on some sort of river obstruction. Jerry pulled up his raft and met with the man on the other raft to try to sort out the problem. When Jerry's suggestion as to how to get the stuck raft moving was rejected because the other man was afraid he would fall in the river and get wet, Jerry promptly pitched him into the river, saying to him that he did not have to be afraid of getting wet now. They then solved the problem and floated both rafts down the river.

Another time Jerry, who was a large man, was cooking up a batch of home brew, naturally for his own consumption, as was the custom among all families in the area, when someone bet him he could not pick up one of the filled barrels and drink from it, thinking that its weight was too much for any man to pick up. Not being any ordinary man, Jerry wrapped his arms around the barrel and, with a heave, picked it up, lifted it to his lips, and calmly took a sip—or two.

He was also a compassionate man. The story is told of "Pony" Collins, so called because he rode off on a pony to join the Confederate Army. Pony was from a poor family and merely a boy when he joined, but he survived. When he returned from the war he had no land on which to settle down and rear a family. Jerry then gave him 50 acres of land on which Pony settled, farmed and built a small home. That home was still standing, vacant and deteriorating, in the midst of other Coleman lands as late as 1950.

Jerry was very supportive of his children, and, like his father, he made gifts of land to them or sold them other pieces, probably at below market prices. In 1881 he sold to his daughter Mary Ann 262 acres for $264 as well as 125 acres for $487 in 1896 after she married to Wallace. In 1896 for love and affection, he deeded over 125 acres to his daughter Elizabeth, who was married to G. W. Williams. He sold to his daughter Missouri, married to Josh Collins, 236 acres for $400 in 1885 and then gave them 126 acres in 1896, also for love and affection. G. W. Collins, Sarah's husband, purchased 73 acres for $125 in 1889. Two properties were transferred to his youngest son and namesake, Jeremiah, Jr.: 332 acres for $483 in 1886 and 132.5 acres free in 1887. Records do not show any transfers to his other two sons, Daniel and James; however, Jerry may have used other means to assist them.

Jerry and Elizabeth were members of the Connors Baptist Church near Cobbtown, where he was a deacon for many years. It is said he had a favorite seat near one of the windows where he could dispose of the juice of his chewing tobacco. He was an active Mason, and his headstone bears the Masonic symbol. He died on February 17, 1914, at the age of 90, the same year World War 1 began. He had lived through three wars—the Mexican American War, the Civil War and the Spanish American War, but he would miss that big one. Elizabeth preceded him in death, dying on June 24, 1889. Both were originally buried on their property but in 1946 family members relocated their headstones to the Sunlight Cemetery in Cobbtown where they can be seen today.

Children of James Jeremiah Coleman and Elizabeth Holland

1. Mary Ann, b. Dec 9, 1850; d. May 11, 1931; m. 1st Sim Wallace and 2nd Houston Kennedy
2. **Daniel Wade, Feb 1, 1852; d. Feb 14, 1921; m. 1st Emma Evaline Tillman on Nov 5, 1874** and 2nd Nellie Martin on Mar 18, 1902.
3. James Frank, b. Oct 31, 1853; d. Jul 17, 1901; m. Mattie J. Gibson on Mar 13, 1879. He died in a drowning accident on Coleman Lake, trying to save the life of his eighteen year old son

who also drowned. Years later his descendants had the bridge over the Ohoopee River on Highway 152 named the James Coleman Bridge.

4. Sarah, b. Jan 16, 1855; d. Dec 4, 1933; m. George W. Collins on Mar 4, 1874.

5. Missouri, b. Nov 15, 1858; d. Aug 11, 1909; m. Josiah C. Collins on Feb 24, 1881

6. Elizabeth, b. Sep 12, 1860; d. May 11, 1933; m. G. M. (Bud) Williams on Feb 2, 1882

7. Jeremiah, Jr. b. Dec 20, 1865; d. Oct 1, 1941; m. Margaret V. Anderson on Oct, 1889. He reared a large family on his farm near Cobbtown and many of the Colemans who still live there are his descendants. Jeremiah, Jr.'s youngest son, Milton Eugene, settled in Valdosta, Georgia, and he and his children Buddy and Vann became close to the descendants of Jeremiah, Jr.'s brother Daniel Wade who had settled in Valdosta as well.

Daniel Wade Coleman

Daniel Wade Coleman, called Dan, was born on Feb 1, 1852, on his father's farm near Cobbtown in Tattnall County, Georgia and died on Feb 14, 1921, in Harrison County, Mississippi. He was the son of James Jeremiah (Jerry) Coleman and wife Elizabeth Holland. Dan married Emma Evaline Tillman on Nov 5, 1874, in Tattnall County. Emma was born on Oct 10, 1857, in Tattnall County and died there on Jun 4, 1899. Her parents were James and Sarah Everett Tillman. Both Dan and Emma are buried in Mt. Zion Cemetery in Toombs County, Georgia. After the death of his wife in 1899, he moved to Harrison County, Mississippi along with ten of his twelve children who were still minors; the two eldest children, having already married, remained in Georgia.

Dan had a large amount of farm and timber land in Tattnall County, part of which he had inherited from his mother's estate and part of which he had purchased although the actual amount is not known. He may also have been given some property by his father although there are no such records. He farmed and also became heavily involved in the turpentine industry. Over time Dan was unable to hold on to much of this property. Court records show that in 1879 he borrowed $500 from J. K. Clarke, giving as security 500 acres located to the east of Ohoopee River. When he was unable to repay this debt, the Sheriff seized his property which was auctioned off. He also borrowed $550 from a Mr. Perry that same year which was secured by a 407 acre tract to the northeast of the same river. That, too, was auctioned off and apparently he sustained large losses on both. These were only two of many legal actions filed against Dan and probably led to his decision to leave Georgia for greener pastures; he was broke and needed a new start. His son Ernest spoke disapprovingly of his father, saying that he was a poor businessman, which, as history shows, Ernest was not.

Dan moved west, probably in late 1899 or early 1900, arriving in Harrison County, Mississippi, in time for the 1900 census takers to record him there. A story passed down by some of Dan's descendants who live in Mississippi is that he had planned to move with his children to Texas but that he was side tracked by the 1900 hurricane that razed Galveston and other parts of South Texas, so he decided to remain in the Gulfport area. Census records show he was living in a boarding house on the Gulf of Mexico, adjacent to the present day Gulfport Presbyterian Church. The 1900 census also identifies Dan as a "turpentine manufacturer." Two young men, James Mathews, twenty six, and William Currie, twenty, identified as "laborers, turpentine orchards," were living in Dan's house as well. Since they both came from Georgia, they may have traveled with the Colemans and were working for or with Dan in the business. Later Currie would start his own turpentine operation in nearby McHenry, and Dan's son Ernest would work for a while for him, learning more about the turpentine business

In 1902 Dan married Nellie Martin, a Harrison County school teacher. Later Dan and his large family moved to a home in Martin's Landing in Handsboro (now a part of Gulfport) which was on property owned by her family. During his time in Mississippi, Dan farmed as well as managed turpentine camps. He also worked as a range rider for the Southern Lumber Company, helping to oversee the management of its vast land holdings.

All of Dan's sons by his first marriage were involved in the naval stores industry. They tapped pine trees for the gum, processed it into turpentine and then sold the turpentine in bulk for commercial and industrial purposes. A "turpentine camp" is where a turpentine producer's still and related facilities were located. Dan's oldest son, Walter, set up his turpentine camp in Tattnall County in an area that is now part of Toombs County. He was the only one of the children to remain his entire life in the area where all of Dan and Emma's children were born.

Children of Daniel Wade Coleman and Emma Evaline Tillman

1. Walter Erastus, b. Nov 1, 1876; d. Nov 30, 1961; m. Ida Jane Carr on Jul 13, 1899. Like his brothers he was involved in the turpentine industry and lived in the Tattnall/Toombs County area all his life. He and his wife are buried in Mt. Zion Cemetery in Toombs County.

2. Margaret, b. Dec 28, 1877; d. Nov 15, 1956; m. Lucian Q. Thompson on Feb 8, 1899, in Tattnall County and moved with him to Pahokee in Palm County, Florida. Both are buried in the Port Mayaca Cemetery in Martin County, Florida.

3. James Jeremiah (J. J.), b. Aug 26, 1879; d. Dec 30, 1924 in Union County, Florida; m. Margaret Ladner on Jan 30, 1910, in Pearl County, Mississippi. Margaret died, date unknown, after giving birth to five children. Afterwards he married Nisey Hewitt on Feb 2, 1924, in Union County, Florida; no known children. J. J. lived in Bay County, Florida, for many years where he managed a large turpentine operation near the town of Betts. It was at the train station there in 1917 that he got into a heated argument with a Bay County Deputy Sheriff. Words led to fisticuffs, with J.J. eventually seizing the Deputy's pistol and shooting him. J. J. did not flee the scene and surrendered to authorities. Still he was convicted of murder and sentenced to life in prison. In 1921 Florida's Governor gave him an unconditional pardon, presumably for the reason that his action was in self-defense. In fact the case might not have gone to trial had the victim been other than a law officer. In 1924 J. J. was murdered in Union County, Florida, where he was then living. No one was convicted of his killing

although some have surmised that he was killed by relatives of the slain deputy sheriff. He is buried in the Lake Butler Cemetery in Union County. The turpentine business was a tough one.

4. Maude Elizabeth, b. Feb 16, 1882; d. Sep 25, 1918, in Washington, DC; never married. She was a nurse, having trained at Charity Hospital in New Orleans. She joined the US Navy on Jun 1, 1917, and was posted to the Navy Hospital in Washington, DC. She died there of influenza and was buried at Arlington National Cemetery in Grave #1, Section 21. Records show that she was the first person buried in this cemetery section which had been set up specifically for military personnel in the medical field. Her headstone reads, "Maude E. Coleman, Nurse, USN."

5. Catherine (Kate) Sarah, b. Jul 1, 1883; d. unknown. In a letter from one of Ira Coleman daughters, Katheryn, in response to my inquiry in 1999, stated that "Daddy always said she married someone the family disapproved of. She told them they would never be bothered with them. She and her husband left and no one ever heard from her. They did not know where she went." Nor do we know today.

6. Ira Geiger, b. Mar 11, 1885; d. Jan 26, 1949; m. Claire Tyson on Dec 20, 1920, in Clarke County, Alabama. He owned a large naval stores operation near the town of Godwinsville, just south of Eastman in Dodge County, Georgia, which included sixteen houses, a commissary and two turpentine stills. He served on the Eastman City Council and lived in a large home in Eastman that still stands. They are both buried in Woodlawn Cemetery in Eastman.

7. Daniel Ernest, b. Aug 17, 1886; d. Jan 14, 1971 in Valdosta, Georgia; m. Alice Viola Hargrove on Dec 24, 1906 in Dodge County, Georgia.

8. Leila Bell (Lela), b. Apr 15, 1888; d. May 4, 1974; never married. She changed the spelling of her first name to Lela. She trained as a nurse at the same hospital as her sister Maude and also joined the US Navy during WWI although it is not known where she worked before or during the war. After the war she decided to remain in the military, serving as chief nurse in Navy hospitals in Pearl Harbor, Chicago and other posts. She retired in San Diego, California, where she took in and reared four of her brother, J. J.'s, orphans. She retired as a Lt (jg) in the Navy and is buried in the "Terrace of Honor" at El Camino Cemetery in San Diego.

9. Clyde Collins, b. Jul 25, 1889; d. Dec 10, 1969; m. Emma Patrick. Not much is known about Clyde except that he worked in the turpentine industry, finally settling in Quitman, Brooks County, Georgia, where he is buried beside his brother Tillman in Oak Lawn Cemetery. He also served in the military during WWI. On his death certificate it is stated that he was separated from his wife.

10. Tillman Eugene, b. Mar 17, 1891; d. Nov 27, 1955; m. Grace Pedigo, and lived in Newton County, Texas, before moving back to Georgia, where he died. His death certificate states that he was divorced from Grace. Like his brothers, he worked in the turpentine industry.

11. Viola Mae (Ola), b. Sep 22, 1892; d. Sep 9, 1921; m. Walter S. Suber in Bay County, Florida. She moved to Port Arthur, Texas. where she died at the tender age of twenty eight of typhoid fever,

leaving four young children behind. Ola is buried in the Port Arthur City Cemetery.

12. Mattie Effie (Martha), b. Jul 7, 1894; d. Jul 12, 1990; m. 1st George Haygood and 2nd a Mr. Jackson. She legally changed her name to Martha. Like her two sisters, she trained as a nurse at Charity Hospital. In 1917 she was among the ten nurses at Touro Hospital in Port Arthur, where she was then working, who signed up to serve with the US Army during WWI. She was assigned to Evacuation Hospital #6 and sent to Juilly, France, which is northeast of Paris. Many American casualties from the Battles of Chateau Thierry and Meuse-Argonnes were evacuated to this 250 bed hospital. When the war ended Martha joined the U. S. Public Health Service, where she was a nurse at the Franklin School, a boarding school for Native Americans in Port Arthur. In 1931 she took a position as a nurse at the Jicarilla Apache Indian Reservation in Cuba, New Mexico, serving there for six years. After retiring from the nursing profession, she lived with her sister Lela in San Diego. When Lela died Martha moved to a nursing home in Boise, Idaho, which was close to the home of a niece, Margaret Coleman, the daughter of Jim Coleman, her nephew and J.J.'s son. She died at the age of ninety six and is buried in Boise.

13. There is also an unnamed child, b. Jun 17, 1896; d. Nov 29, 1896, who is buried beside his/her parents in Mt. Zion Cemetery.

After Daniel's first wife died, Dan married Sara Ellen "Nellie" Martin on March 19, 1902, in Harrison County, Mississippi. They had two children. She died on December 9, 1933 and is buried in the Old Handsboro Cemetery in Gulfport.

14. Mollie O., b. Dec 20, 1902; d. Oct 30, 1994; m. 1st Luther White Ruble in Harrison County, Mississippi, and 2nd J. R. Hickman in Stone County, Mississippi.

15. John Wade (Jack), b. Apr 26, 1906; d. Jun 21, 1967; never married. He was a school teacher, coach and principal.

Daniel Ernest Coleman

Daniel Ernest Coleman, called by most D. E. and by his wife, Ernest, was born in the small town of Ohoopee in that part of Tattnall County that is now Toombs County. In the late 1890s he moved with his father and most of his siblings to Harrison County, Mississippi, where he attended public and private schools in and around Poplarville. He completed high school and received a teaching certificate but never taught school. Most of the information about his early days in Mississippi is contained in a profile written about him in *Georgia through Two Centuries*, Volume 2. His full page photograph is also included with the profile.

After completing school Ernest helped his father in his turpentine camp. He then worked for W. L. Currie of McHenry, Mississippi, in his turpentine operations where he was paid $30 a month but had to pay back $8 of that amount for room and board. He received a paycheck only twice a year: Christmas and July the 4th. Later he worked for a while in his brother Jim's turpentine camp before moving to Eastman, Georgia, to work with another brother, I. G., in this same type of business. In 1906 Ernest met and married an Eastman girl, Alice Viola Hargrove; he was twenty, she was nineteen. Their marriage was performed by A. G. Brown, minister of the Gospel, and is recorded in Dodge County, Georgia, Marriage Book D.

Alice, who was born near Eastman on February 24, 1887, about six months after her husband, was descended from a prominent Dodge County family. Her parents were Larkin L. and Elizabeth Hamilton Hargrove. Her grandfather was a farmer and a Baptist minister while her father was a respected businessman and farmer who had joined the Georgia Militia at the age of sixteen and had fought at the Battle of Atlanta. Her mother was a Hamilton, a pioneer family in this section of Georgia whose sons and daughters were respected leaders and citizens in Dodge County and many of the surrounding counties.

While her family was far from wealthy in those post-Civil War years, Alice led a relatively comfortable life and received a good, if basic, education. Their well-built and attractive home at 305 Bethel Street in Eastman where her parents lived later in life burned in 2010. Alice's daughter-in-law, Corinne Coleman, tells the following story: "Once at the funeral of a relative someone told me of the first time she had seen Alice, when Alice was a young, unmarried lady. She remarked on her petite beauty. I am sure she must have been pretty and tiny."

By the age of twenty two Ernest had gained enough experience to establish his own turpentine production business. He formed a partnership with W. T. McGowan of Mobile, Alabama, to work a timber tract for turpentine production which was located fifty miles north of Mobile near the town of Carlton, a very remote community. There were no roads to the site and the only means of communication with the "outside" world was by steamboat on the Alabama River which came about once a week to the port nearest to his turpentine camp. Ernest and Alice had planned to spend the Christmas of 1908 back in Georgia with their family, but, when they missed the boat, they had to remain in Alabama because there was no alternative route out of the area.

Alice gave birth to her first child, Hargrove, in Carlton, with the help of a midwife. The nearest doctor was many miles away. When Hargrove was unable to suckle properly, Alice had no idea what to do until an old black woman diagnosed the condition as "thrush mouth" and provided a remedy. Alice once commented on this event by saying that the nearest white person was fifty miles away. Ernest decided to terminate the partnership after one year, at least, in part, because of the remoteness of the area and the difficulties Alice was having in rearing her child. Moreover, Alice became pregnant again in mid-1909 and decided she was not going to have another baby in such an isolated and primitive part of the world.

Alice probably departed for Georgia in the fall of 1909 while Ernest remained to collect and sell the "scrape" which is the gum coating that dries on the scarified "face" of the pine tree and is collected in the winter months after the end of the turpentine production season. After settling his accounts, Ernest arrived in Oak Park, Georgia, in Bulloch County near the Coleman family home place, in the early part of 1910, where Alice had settled in to give birth to their second son, Theo.

Between 1910 and 1919 Ernest worked in various turpentine camps in the Southeast, mostly in Georgia. Sometimes he worked for others; sometimes he had his own turpentine camp. By 1914 the family had relocated to Hahira in Lowndes County where his daughter, Evelyn, was born. In 1916 they relocated to a home in

23

Blue Springs, Brooks County, just over the line from Lowndes County. Records show that in November 1916 Ernest leased 5,060 acres of land in Lowndes County "for the purpose of cupping, working and using said timber for turpentine purposes." He paid $1,500 for the one-year lease which he assigned to the Downing Company, a "factor" in Brunswick.

Factoring is a type of financing arrangement whereby the factor provides the necessary capital and operating funds for the turpentine producer to carry out his operations, and, in return, the factor receives the first proceeds from the sale of the turpentine products until the loan with interest is repaid. In many cases the only profit the producer might realize would be from the winter "scraping." Ernest never really found a satisfactory working arrangement until 1919 when he began working for a half interest in a well-organized turpentine organization owned by the Mallory Brothers in Quitman, Georgia, who were related to him through his mother's family, the Tillmans. By 1926 he had paid for his partnership interest and bought out his partners.

Records show that as early as 1920 he had settled on some land in Mineola, a railroad station and unincorporated town just off Highway 41 between Valdosta and Hahira. There, not far from the railroad tracks, he built his home, a workers' commissary, worker quarters and a turpentine still. He was retained as the Mineola station master for the Georgia Southern Railroad as well as appointed the local postmaster, both of which he operated out of his commissary. Originally he had built the commissary to the east of the railroad tracks, but after that building burned, he rebuilt it to the west of the tracks just across from his home.

The road in front of his house is still named Coleman Road, and today it leads past his old home to Stone Creek, the large housing development and golf course built by Young Tillman on land owned by the Tillman family. A small part of this development around the main gate was purchased from Ernest's heirs so that the development would have frontage on Coleman Road. All the turpentine buildings and facilities in Mineola have been demolished and replaced by private houses. Their old home still stands and is occupied, although it has been modified somewhat. Unfortunately, the big screened-in front porch where everyone loved to sit and chat has been removed.

Ernest continued to buy and lease land for his turpentine operations. Along with the timber land he acquired some cleared land for farming, but it was clear that his primary occupation was turpentine. Over time he would acquire more than 3,000 acres of land of which 2,200 acres would still be under his ownership at the time of his death. When he died in 1971 he owed over $100,000 in estate taxes, which gives an indication of the value of his assets, nearly all of which were in land.

The arrival of the Depression greatly affected the turpentine industry and with it, Ernest and Alice's fortunes. During the worst days of the Depression, the area between their home and the railroad was covered with barrels of turpentine, ready for a sale that seemed unlikely. At that time Alice was said to have had trouble finding enough money to buy a 3 cent postage stamp. But they had enough food, and Ernest had some cash income from his positions as postmaster and station master.

There is one story that Ernest liked to tell that typifies both those Depression days in general and the turpentine business in particular. A turpentine man saw a worker spill a small amount of gum on the floor of the still, and he was apparently going to leave it there. The owner admonished the worker to pick it up saying, "that tablespoon of gum is my profit." Ernest gave credit to poor families in the neighborhood to purchase food and other commodities at his commissary. In turn the A.S. Pendleton Company, a wholesale grocer in Valdosta, gave Ernest the credit he needed. (Lowndes Shaw, whose daughter would later marry their son Theo, was a charter shareholder and one-time director of the Pendleton Company). This kind of treatment given to needy people in his neighborhood would allow Ernest to develop a local political base. Turpentine began to pay off once again in the waning years of the Depression when preparations for WWII began, and the family fortunes improved considerably as turpentine became a much needed commodity for the war effort.

Ernest was an early, perhaps a charter, member of the American Turpentine Farmers Association Cooperative (ATFA, a Southern based trade association headquartered in Valdosta. He also served for several years on its board of directors. At its peak, the ATFA's membership consisted of some 4,500 turpentine producers and farmers, nearly all in the Southeast. One of the annual highlights of this association was the beauty contest to elect "Miss Gum Spirits of Turpentine," a highly sought after prize among the local belles. His grandsons Dan and Wade Coleman carried with them small sample bottles of turpentine, with the ATFA label attached, to the 1953 Boy Scout Jamboree in Irving, California, to trade for souvenirs with other scouts.

During those same post-war years, the traditional turpentine industry began to decline as cheaper imports, new methods of extraction, and synthetic materials made the business, as Ernest and others in the South practiced it, non-competitive. By the late 1950s Ernest and his sons had closed down their operation. Accordingly, as more producers and farmers left the business, ATFA's membership dwindled until finally, in the 1980s, the association ceased to exist. Coincidently, Wade Coleman, who had traded turpentine bottles at the Jamboree, would be the last attorney retained to handle the legal affairs of the then defunct ATFA.

Ernest also had numerous outside business interests. For many years he was a director of the Citizen's Bank of Hahira which was owned then and today by the Hollis family. He was a shareholder and director of Carson McLane, Inc., a funeral home business still operated by the McLane family. Ernest was also active in civic affairs. In 1932 he was elected to the Lowndes County School Board and served in that capacity for twelve years, of which eleven years were as chairman of the board. In 1945 he was elected to a four-year term on the Lowndes County Board of Commissioners, serving as chairman throughout that term. He declined to run again believing that one term in that trying position was enough. During WWII he served on the Selective Service Board, also referred to as the Draft Board. In that capacity he had the onerous duty of sending young men to war, including all three of his sons, who thankfully survived. He also was at one time chairman of the local Democratic Party Committee.

During his tenure as a County Commissioner, the Valdosta Municipal Airport was constructed and his name as one of the commissioners appears on a memorial plaque at the entrance of the old airport terminal building. His picture appeared in the

Valdosta Daily Times one day when he and the other commissioners were shown boarding the first commercial airline flight from the new Valdosta airport to Atlanta. This may have been his first ever flight.

Ernest was especially active in the Shrine Temple. Membership in the Shriners consists of Masons who have already reached its highest level of achievement, the 32nd degree. Each Shrine temple covered a larger geographic area where separate local Shrine clubs would be set up for meeting purposes and to hold events for local members or nobles. Ernest was a member of Hasan Temple of the Shrine of Albany, Georgia, which covered Valdosta. On several different occasions Ernest was elected president of the Valdosta Shrine Club, and in 1949 he provided a site on his property near the Withlacoochee River for the construction of a Shrine club. In addition to serving its members, the building also functioned for many years as a social events venue because it had a large open meeting room that was perfect for dances, proms and such. Most young people growing up in the 1950s in Valdosta remember it well. The building burned in about 1960 and the land reverted to Ernest's ownership. Today this site is part of a housing community, River Chase, which was developed in the 1980s by two of his grandsons, Stephen and Richard Coleman.

His other social memberships included the Woodmen of the World and the Benevolent and Protective Order of Elks. He was a life-long Baptist and served as a deacon of the Lee Street Baptist Church in Valdosta for over twenty years. His will included a substantial bequest to his church.

What were Ernest and Alice like? His descendants remember Ernest as a stern, serious man who was strict with himself and his family, particularly his sons. He was a hard businessman, yet he had to be hard to survive such a rough business. It is said that he slept with a pistol under his pillow so as to be ready to protect his family from the tough and sometimes reckless men he had hired to work in his turpentine camps. He was not known to drink hard stuff, but he did have a penchant for big cigars. In fact his clothes and his surroundings always smelled strongly of tobacco. He was all business and, to his grandsons, somewhat aloof and unapproachable. But his grandsons never recall his being unkind or angry with them. To his grandsons he was Granddaddy; no cute name for him.

Probably because he started out in life with almost nothing, he was very careful with money. His life style remained simple even after it was clear that he had become fairly well-to-do. His home in Mineola was much more modest than would be expected of someone of his eventual position and wealth. Yet he provided a good home and educated his children to the degree they wanted to be educated, including sending two sons to a prep school near Atlanta before their university education.

Alice had been thrown unprepared into the rough and tumble world of turpentine camps, but somehow she learned to cope. What she was not able to cope with was the early death of her only daughter, Evelyn, who died a few days before she turned twenty one. It had a terrible effect on Alice, and for months after her death she went to her grave site daily, spending hours there. She became old before her time. Her church was her only interest outside of her family. Living in rural Mineola she did not have any other outside interests such as clubs or women's groups. She stayed in touch with her brothers and sisters from the Eastman area who periodically would drop by her home for a visit. Neither she nor Ernest ever took a real vacation even when money was not an issue. Together they had made it through some tough times and money was not a commodity to be squandered. Their only personal indulgence was to trade in for a new car every two years, usually a big Buick.

After closing down his turpentine business, Ernest focused on his farming operations but his eyesight began to fail. He had several eye operations but eventually he went almost completely blind. In a letter to her niece, Dorothy Hargrove Stoeger, Alice writes, "I can't plan anything more. Even tho Ernest is much better, it still takes a lot of care. His retirement has not been restful and he still worries about business. He can't see to drive a car and it gets on his nerves to depend on others." Finally, looking after him became too much for her so he went into a nursing home and later died in the hospital at the age of eighty four.

Alice remained in their home after his death, but eventually she moved into a nursing home as well. During her last years she corresponded with her nieces and saw her various grandchildren (she had eight), daughters-in-law and friends who visited. In a letter to Dorothy shortly after Ernest died, she says, "You will be surprised how I remember the past, even things that happened when I was a barefoot child. Sometimes I think I need more to occupy my mind but since he's gone, there isn't much to do but think." Obviously she loved and missed her husband very much. In another letter she writes, "I think I will get well in time but my age is against me. If only I had a daughter. I see daughters here giving their old mothers such loving care, I can't help but be sad. However this is my portion in life and I try not to argue with God. I miss Ernest and Hargrove more than words can express. They were the ones I could lean on when things got beyond me." It is clear that she was still thinking about her long dead daughter as well as the son who had lived next door to her most of his adult life and, of course, her husband of sixty five years.

Because her eyesight also declined with age, the loneliness of old age was even less bearable. She had outlived her four children by many years. By the time of her death at the age of ninety four, she was almost blind. Old age had not been kind to either of them. Both died essentially of the infirmities of their age. They are buried in Valdosta's Sunset Hill Cemetery in the same plot with their son Hargrove and his wife and their only daughter.

Children of Daniel Ernest Coleman and Alice Viola Hargrove

1. Ernest Hargrove (Hargrove), b. Nov 18, 1908; d. Dec 2, 1969, m. Lucy Cary Robinson on Oct 1, 1938. Hargrove worked with his father in the turpentine business for many years before starting his own operation. He graduated from Valdosta High School and attended Mercer University but never finished. He joined the Army Air Corps in WWII and served as a sergeant with the 334th Bomber Squadron, 95th Bomber Group in England. They did not have any children.

2. **Theo Wade, b. Apr 1, 1910; d. Feb 17, 1960; m. Meta Aubrey Shaw on Nov 12, 1938.**

3. Evelyn Christine, b. Mar 10, 1913; d. Mar 4, 1934; never married. She was attending Andrew College in Cuthbert, Georgia. when she died.

4. Daniel Earl (Earl) b. Feb 25, 1922; d. May 2, 1977; m. Corinne Fuller DeLoach on May 29, 1949. Earl graduated from Georgia Military Academy before attending the University of Georgia where he received a Bachelor's degree in forestry. He then began working for the North Carolina Forestry Service. At his father's request he relocated to Mineola in 1950 to work with his father in the turpentine business. Once they closed down this business he taught at Lowndes High School until he retired in 1975, two years before his death. Earl served in the Army Air Force in WWII as a B17 Engineer Gunner in the European Theater of Operations, flying twenty five missions over occupied Europe. He and Corinne had three children: Jane, Daniel and David.

The Tillman Lineage

The history of the Tillman's or Tilghman, as it was spelled in some family names, can be traced back to its very early origins in England. The first known Tilghman in this line was Johannes or John Tilghman who was born about 1225 into an ancient family living in Snodland Parish, County Kent, although there are some records of a Tilghman family living in that county as early as 690. The Tilghman's were "Thanes," a title reserved for men who were rewarded for their services to the King by gifts of land. Their distinction rested not so much on hereditary rank but on services rendered. But, in the end, they became nobility exceeding that of the Earls. They became ealdormen, bishops and judges. The family owned Holloway Court in County Kent which was built about 1300 and existed until 1659.

Christopher Tilghman, who died in the early part of the seventeenth century, married Anna Sanders, the daughter of Edward and Anna Pandreth Sanders. English records indicate Anna was a direct descendant of William the Conqueror. Christopher's son, also named Christopher, was born in Selling, Faversham, County Kent, in about 1600 and married Ruth Devonshire there. He was the first Tilghman in our line to immigrate to the New World, arriving in Accomac County, Virginia, on May 9, 1635. Accomac is located on the lower tip of the eastern shore of the Chesapeake Bay. He died in James City County, Virginia.

The son of this Christopher, Gideon, was born in Accomac County, Virginia, but moved to the Manokin region of the eastern shore between 1663 and 1666. The area is located in Somerset County, Maryland, north of Accomac. Records reveal that he was a member of the Church of England. Gideon was also a farmer as well as a cattle man. His cattle mark was registered on November 10, 1669, with the county court as follows, "Underbitted of both ears cropt of both ears two slits of the right ear and one slitt of the left." Now he could locate those cattle that were left to roam the woods. He must have had a good sense of humor since he gave his land holdings such names as "Tilghman's Adventure," "Small Hope," and "Gideon's Luck," all in Somerset County.

Gideon's son, John Stephen Tillman, was born in Somerset County on September 15, 1689, and located his plantation there at a place called "Tillman's Lott". He married Rosanna Tapper, had three sons, and died on March 26, 1732. He changed the spelling of the family name to Tillman which is more commonly used today in most of southeastern states. His youngest son, also named John,

33

moved to North Carolina before the Revolutionary War and, after the war, to Georgia. It is this Tillman and his descendants that are discussed below.

John Tillman

Born in 1731 in Somerset County, John Tillman, the son of John Stephen Tillman, was first noted in records when he served as a sixteen year old soldier in the Colonial militia in 1747. It is believed that he had a first wife but there is no record of any marriage or any children. However, at the age of forty three, he did marry Sarah Eggerton who was twenty nine years his junior and who bore him seven children. By 1761 the family had moved to Craven County, North Carolina, where he purchased some land. One deed states that he bought "300 acres in the county on the south side of the Trent River, joining near Running Brand." Another deed states he bought "250 acres on the south side of Southwest Creek, including the place he lives in."

John played a major role during the Revolutionary War period. He was a representative from Craven County in the 5th Provincial Congress of the State of North Carolina, which was held over a four-week period in November and December 1776. Then, in seven different years between 1777 and 1795, he served as a member of the Assembly of North Carolina representing Craven County. He also served many years as a justice of the peace beginning in 1777. That same year he was named to the Committee of Public Accounts. On April 22, 1776, he was appointed to the grade of 2nd Major by the North Carolina Provincial Congress. On April 30, 1778, he was assigned to command Fort Hancock. To take this job he resigned his seat in the State Assembly. John was promoted to the grade of Colonel of the Craven County Militia on November 18, 1779, replacing Col. John Bryan. He held that rank as late as November 1786. In a newspaper advertisement on July 2, 1791, John offers himself as a candidate for the North Carolina Senate. In another ad on June 26, 1794, he thanks his constituency for electing him once again to represent them. Finally records show that he was appointed as a Commissioner of Navigation and Pilotage for New Bern, a major port in North Carolina.

Around 1800, now a much older man of some sixty nine years, he moved to Bulloch County, Georgia, where he lived until 1829, dying at the advanced age of ninety eight. His widow died in 1845. Their burial place is unknown, but it is probably on the land that his son Joseph later owned.

Children of John Tillman and Sarah Eggerton

1. James, b. Nov 16, 1776; d. Dec 14, 1855, m. Martha Marlow in 1800.

2. John, b. 1777; d. unk

3. Mary, b. 1780; d. unk; m. Henry Simmons on Mar 4, 1800.

4. Elizabeth, b. 1781, d. unk; m. William Rushing on Mar 12, 1801.

5. Nancy, b. 1782, d. unk; m. Daniel Simmons on Mar 17, 1811

6. Henry, b. Feb 22, 1790; d. Mar 17, 1851; m. Aleph Simmons on Sep 13, 1816.

7. **Joseph Isaiah, b. Jan 6, 1792; d. May 5, 1845; m. 1st Catherine Chewning on Mar 17, 1816 and 2nd Cassandra Everett on Jun 2, 1831.**

Joseph Tillman

Joseph Tillman arrived with his parents in Georgia when he was still very young. He then moved to Tattnall County around 1810 where his name appeared on the county's jury list that year. He was only eighteen at the time. During the War of 1812 he served for two years as an ensign (lieutenant) in the 1st Georgia Militia Regiment. Later, he served as a state senator from his county for the 1827-1828 term and later as a delegate from Tattnall to the State Anti-Tariff Convention in 1832. In 1839 he served as a captain of militia in his military district.

By the early 1820s Joseph had begun to acquire land on the Canoochee River, along that stretch where the river meets Cedar Creek and Dry Creek. Usually these purchases took the form of headright grants on land that he had already occupied and surveyed. His largest acquisition took place on June 6, 1836, when he was granted title to 2,673 acres. By the time of his death he owned about 5,000 acres of farm and timber lands in Tattnall County and another 1,500 acres in adjoining counties. He had a workforce of some twenty five slaves to help him. After his death in 1845 his estate administrators valued his properties at $22,915, a considerable sum for that time.

Joseph and his family lived in a fine two-story home on a 950 acre tract located on the banks of the Canoochee River. In 1829 he constructed a toll-bridge across the Canoochee River close to his home. The Tattnall County Inferior Court, which had to approve this development, also set the rates he could charge as follows: 43 ¾ cents for a 2 wheeled carriage; 25 cents for each road wagon; 12 ½ cents for each man on a horse; 43 ¾ cents for each horse and cart; 6 ¼ cents for each person on foot; 6 ¼ cents for a horse; 3 cents for each cattle; 2 cents for a hog, sheep or goat.

In 1829 Joseph was appointed by the Inferior Court of Tattnall County as one of three commissioners "to review the public utility of a road from or near Joseph Tillman to intersect the Savannah Road at or near Edward Kennedy and mark out the same and report both to the Court." He also served a number of terms as a commissioner of roads in Capt. Durrance's Militia District.

Joseph first married Catherine Chewning in 1816 with whom he had four children. Two of his sons, James and Henry, married daughters of John Carter Everett. After Catherine died in 1830 he married Cassandra Everett, who was a sister of the same John Carter Everett, and they had four children. As a result of this second marriage Cassandra became the stepmother of James and Henry as well as their aunt owing to the marriage of the two young Tillman men to her nieces.

He died at his home and is buried beside his first wife, Catherine, in the family cemetery (now lost) on his property. Once her husband's estate was settled, his second wife, Cassandra, moved to Thomas County, Georgia, with her four young children. She died in 1864 and is buried in the Everett Family Cemetery near Boston, Georgia.

The first four children on this list were born to Joseph and his first wife, Catherine, while the last four were born to him and his second, Cassandra. Note that four of their eight children married children from the Everett family.

Children of Joseph Tillman and Catherine Chewning (1-4); and Cassandra Everett (5-8)

1. James, b. Oct 8, 1817; d. Sep 15, 1870; m. Sarah Everett on Sep 3, 1840.

2. Sarah, b. Jul 18, 1819; d. Mar 19, 1867; m 1st Aaron Barber Everett on Jan 28, 1836 and 2nd Perry Collins on May 1849.

3. Henry, b. July 1820; d. Mar 22, 1877; m. 1st Susan Everett on Nov 22, 1840 and 2nd Jane Williams on Jul 25, 1843. He formed a company of soldiers at the beginning of the Civil War and was elected their captain. This was Company D, comprised of men from Bulloch County, and it was assigned to the 61st Georgia Infantry in Evan's Brigade with Army of Virginia. In September 1862 he was promoted to Major and apparently assigned to the Regimental staff. Then in January 1863 he was promoted to Lieutenant Colonel but resigned shortly afterwards and returned home. After the war he moved to Taylor County, Florida, where he was an inferior court judge and county sheriff.

4. Susan, b. May 1, 1827; d. Jan 20, 1907; m. Abraham E. Eason, Sr. on Nov 23, 1843.

5. Eliza Everett, b. May 11, 1834; d. Jan 3, 1910; m. 1st Charles E. Groover on Nov 11, 1852 and 2nd John Reynolds.

6. Cassandra, b. Jan 15, 1837; d. Jul 27, 1903; m. Mariner J. Culpepper.

7. Joseph I. Jr., b. Aug 26, 1839; d. Feb 24, 1865; m. Sallie Everett on Jan 5, 1859.

8. John, b. Apr 4, 1845; d. Aug 6 1899; m. 1st Mary L. Wyche on Dec 28, 1868 and 2nd Charlie Gaulden.

James M. Tillman

James Tillman was the oldest son of one of the wealthiest and most respected citizens in Tattnall County. Born in 1817 and raised on a large plantation, he probably had more educational and social advantages than were available to most young men then living in Georgia's rural reaches. Many of the civic positions and activities in which his father was involved were continued by his oldest son.

Early on James was appointed several times as a Commissioner of Roads in the 39th Militia District. He served frequently as a grand juror: 1847, 1856, 1860, 1868 and 1870, the last just before his death. In 1860 he was appointed an overseer of the poor in the Blue Ridge area of the county. In January 1845 he was named the county tax collector and served for two years. From 1847 to 1852 he represented Tattnall County in the Georgia State House of Representatives.

In addition to his civic activities he was both a farmer and a timber man. On September 14, 1853, he attended a meeting of seventeen timber men at Lumber City, Georgia, to discuss matters of mutual interest in their business. Lumber City is where the Oconee and Ocmulgee Rivers meet to form the Altamaha River which leads to the coast at Darien, the destination for most timber products. The Canoochee River, which fronted James' property, bordered one of the most productive timber growing areas of the state, in part because of the density of the longleaf and yellow pines but also because of the numerous rivers that intersected the region thus allowing the timber to be transported easily (for the times) to Darien. It was in James' interest to protect this valuable mode of transportation.

James inherited some land from his father when the latter died in 1845. The county property assessment records show that he owned 1,316 acres of pine lands. In 1850 he worked his land with the assistance of fourteen slaves. By 1860, that number had increased to twenty one, plus three slaves borrowed from other owners. Their value in 1862 was placed at $9,950 but all those slave assets would vanish after the Civil War when the slaves were freed. He must have also grown a substantial amount of cotton which is why he had so many slaves.

When the war broke out he was forty four years old with seven children by then and a large plantation to operate, a big responsibility for a middle aged man. While he was exempt from active military service owning to his age he did enroll in the 1192nd Militia Company in 1864. The enlistment roster recorded that he was forty seven years, five months old, had a double barrel shotgun in good condition, a horse, saddle and bridle. His occupation was listed as farmer. It is not known whether he participated in any of skirmishes that took place with the Union soldiers on their way to Savannah.

One note: the *Tilghman-Tillman Family Register* states that James Tillman served in B Company, 2nd Georgia Infantry during the War. That is not true. County records show he remained in Tattnall County throughout that time, serving only in the militia. In fact the Tattnall County Inferior Court in its April 1863 term appointed James Tillman to appraise the estate of James L. Coleman, deceased in 1862, and then in the September 1863 term to distribute the estate's proceeds, which would not have been possible for James to do if he were away in the army. Records show that another James Tillman (perhaps a distant relative?)

joined the 2nd Georgian Infantry in October 1861 in Manassas, Virginia, and served continuously in the Army of Northern Virginia until his surrender with the unit at Appomattox.

James married Sarah Everett, a daughter of John Carter Everett, with whom he had ten children. James died in 1870, a relatively young man of fifty three, his youngest child being only four years old. Sarah passed away twenty eight years later. Both are buried in the Tillman Family Cemetery in unmarked graves.

Children of James Tillman and Sarah Everett

1. John Everett, b. Feb 21, 1842; d. 1913; m. Elmira Miller on Feb 14, 1861.

2. Catherine, b. Jul 19, 1844; d. May 21, 1871; m. Washington Leonard Geiger on Nov 17, 1858.

3. Elizabeth Everett, b. Apr 10, 1846; d. Nov 11, 1918; m. Josiah Kennedy on Aug 1, 1861.

4. Joseph, b. May 3, 1848; d. Nov 4, 1909; m. Mary Kennedy on Jun 7, 1866.

5. Henry L., b. Mar 16, 1850, d. unk; m. Callie Padgett in 1878.

6. Sarah, b. Jan 6, 1852; d. Jul 15, 1855.

7. Margaret, b. Jun 17, 1854; d. Sep 9, 1929; m. John Weaver on Feb 1872.

8. **Emma Evaline, b. Oct 10, 1857; d. Jun 2, 1899; m. Daniel Wade Coleman on Nov 5, 1874.**

9. James J., b. Jun 8, 1863, d. Jun 5, 1923; m. Nona Belle Anderson on Aug 22, 1888.

10. Leila E., b. Mar 30, 1866; d. unk; m. J. P. Collins.

The Everett Lineage

Alvaretta Kenan Register, an Everett family descendant and well-known genealogist, has written the definitive history of John Everett from North Carolina. She states that the first known Everett in this family line is Nathaniel Everett, who was born in 1678, and moved in 1683 to Morratock in Chowan Precinct (County), North Carolina. His place of birth is not known. On November 4, 1713, the precinct council appointed him as one of four men to appraise an estate. Various precinct records and deeds show Nathaniel as being very active in land transfers and precinct affairs. In 1797 Tyrrell County, North Carolina, was created from several other counties, including Chowan, and Nathaniel's land became a part of this new county. He married Mary, maiden name unknown, and had at least four children. Nathaniel made his will on November 2, 1749, in which he named his children and disposed of this property. He probably died shortly thereafter since his will was probated on December 5, 1749.

One of Nathaniel's sons, also named Nathaniel, was born in 1707 at Kendrick's Creek in Chowan County. He married Elizabeth, maiden name unknown, in about 1727 and settled on land his father had given him after his marriage. He appears frequently in Tyrrell County records, through land purchases and sales, jury service and court appointments. North Carolina records also show that this second Nathaniel served in a foot company of soldiers commanded by Capt. Evan Jones, effective January 17, 1747, for the militia district located between Bark Poplar Swamp and Welches Creek. He remained his entire life in that county where he and his wife raised fifteen children. He made his will on

February 20, 1782, which was probated in July 1782, indicating that he died in the interim period.

The home place for both Nathaniel's, father and son, was on Conniber Creek, also known as Morratock Swamp in Chowan, then Tyrrell County, which is located on the Atlantic Ocean coastline in northern North Carolina. When Nathaniel, the father, deeded this property to his son Nathaniel, "he did deliver the like quiet and peaceable possession of the same, by turff and twig unto Nathaniel Everett." In those days, the seller would actually take something growing or being a part of the land, such as tree branches (twigs) or soil (turff) and hand it to the purchaser, or in this case, it would be done, as an integral part of the transaction, although the transaction would also be put in writing.

John Everett

John Everett was born in about 1743 in Tyrrell County, the son of Nathaniel and Elizabeth Everett. In about 1772 he married Sarah Fagan, the daughter of Bedford and Mary Fagan, and began farming on land his father gave or sold to him. When the Revolutionary War broke out, he claimed to have served periodically with the North Carolina militia for some five years, taking part in various military actions when his unit was called up. After his death his widow applied for a war pension in 1846, and in her application she stated "that in the course of the war, he was wounded in the shoulder by a rifle ball which remained in his shoulder until his death."

According to Sarah this had occurred at Betty's Bridge on Drowning Creek in the Pedee River area. He had served under

Capt. De Jarnette during his war services, and one of his fellow soldiers was James Pickett. She also remembered seeing her husband once in the company of Col. Thomas Wade. Sarah's pension application was rejected, however, insofar as there was no record of his service. That does not mean that he did not serve in the militia, but it does mean that there is insufficient evidence of military service to qualify for membership in, for example, the DAR Book of Patriots or the SAR.

In January 1785 John sold his land in Tyrrell County to Joseph Jones and moved with his family to Effingham County, Georgia, that same year. He received a land grant in that county on November 19, 1791, for 400 acres, which was surrounded by vacant land, and a second nearby 400 acre tract in 1793 which became part of Screven County when in 1794 it was cut out of Effingham. It was on this land that he built his home. Eventually this property became part of Bulloch County when it was created in 1796 and later into Candler County in 1914 when the latter was formed. Like his neighbors John farmed and cut timber; records show that he was the owner of a saw mill as early as 1805. Between 1801 and 1819 he acquired five more tracts of land in Bulloch County totaling 1,460 acres. Three of those tracts were located on Belchers Mill Creek and the other two on Mill Creek.

John was a pioneer settler in Bulloch County and, accordingly, participated in many civic activities in those early days. On June 12, 1798, he was appointed a judge on the county's inferior court and, in this position, was one of the four judges who in 1800 laid out the county seat of Statesboro. In 1799 he was named a justice of the peace. In October 1787 he was named captain of 1st Company, Effingham County Militia. He served later as a lieutenant in the Bulloch County Militia's 47th district from 1804 to 1808. He was commissioned a major in the militia on November 7, 1808, and continued to serve in this position for some four years.

On November 17, 1820, John died in Bulloch County. His will, dated July 29, 1820, was probated that same year but not recorded until the July term in 1828 in the court of the ordinary. He left his estate to his children with his wife, Sarah, having a life interest. His daughter, Hannah, died in 1820, just before her father's death, and her share of his estate was willed to her two children, John and Sarah McCall.

John and Sarah are buried on the old Everett plantation in present day Candler County, Georgia, in the family burial ground. The Everett home place, according to records in Deed Book "A", page 66, was called "Spring Grove," but formerly was known as "Belcher's Old Cowpens" on Belcher's Mill Creek. His widow outlived her husband and all seven of her children, dying on May 24, 1851, at the very old age of 105. She made a nuncupative will which was probated on July 8, 1851, and an administrator was appointed. This was challenged in court, however, and her grandson Jehu Everett was appointed estate administrator. Her total estate of $10,460.93 was divided equally among the heirs of her seven deceased children. Except for Joshua and Hannah all their children moved to other counties and states.

Children of John Everett and Sarah Fagan

1. **Joshua, b. Sep 27, 1774; d. Feb 14, 1846; m. Jane Carter on Oct 7, 1797.**

2. Josiah, b. 1776; d. 1842; m. 1st Eleanor Johnson in 1805 and 2nd Nancy Heath on Dec 3, 1841. He was the surveyor who developed the city plan for Statesboro in 1800. He moved first to Pulaski County, Georgia, before resettling in Leon County, Florida, then to Decatur County, Georgia, where he died.

3. Enoch, b. Jul 6, 1779; d. May 1802; m. Margaret Byrd on Feb 13, 1802. He moved to Liberty County, Georgia, before settling finally in Washington County, Alabama, where he died.

4. Jehu Winott, b. Oct 15, 1780; d. Jan 23, 1847; m. Mary Jones on Mar 18, 1807. He also moved to Washington County, Alabama.

5. Hannah, b. 1782; d. Jun 28, 1805; m. Charles McCall. Hannah married a man who was 50 years her senior; she was his second wife. They had three children, the first born when she was about sixteen, and she probably died giving birth to her third child. Charles was a Revolutionary War veteran and a very large slave owner and planter in Bulloch County. He died about 1815. Alvaretta Kenan Register, the esteemed chronicler of the Everett family, is descended from this line.

6. John Fagan, b. Mar 15, 1784; d. Jun 23, 1842; m. 1st Sarah Ann Lester Mitchell on Jan 26, 1804, 2nd Sarah Hand on Nov 20, 1818, and 3rd Ann Blount Slade on Apr 9, 1838. He settled in Savannah where he founded in January 1802, a semi-weekly newspaper, the Savannah *Republican*. He then moved to Mobile in the then Territory of Alabama where he became a very influential person, which included serving three terms as Mayor. He was a State representative, county judge and a probate judge. John served as a captain of militia during the Indian wars in the early 1800's. His son, Jack Everett, moved to Texas where he came to be known as an intrepid fighter both during the various battles

with Mexico as well as against the Indians. A daughter, Martha, married Robert Leighton Crawford, and their daughter, Frank (her real name and the name of her father's best friend) was the second wife of Commodore Cornelius Vanderbilt, marrying him in 1869 when he was seventy five and she thirty.

7. Aaron, b. 1787; d. 1838; m. Mary Martha Slater on Nov 11, 1811. Aaron moved to Thomas County, Georgia, where he was the surveyor who prepared the plan for Thomasville. Many of his descendants still live in the southwest part of Georgia.

The Vanderbilt Connection

As noted in the text, John Fagan Everett had three wives. The second, Sarah Hand, was the daughter of Obediah Hand, whose sister Phebe Hand, had married Cornelius Van der Bilt. They were the parents of Commodore Cornelius Vanderbilt. John and Sarah Hand Everett had a granddaughter named Frank Crawford (her real name) who became the second wife of the Commodore; he was her first cousin twice removed. John and his first wife, Sarah Mitchell, had another granddaughter, Amelia Townsend, whose husband, Bishop Holland N. Tyerie of Nashville, Tennessee, had started a small college. When Frank married the wealthiest man in America, Frank and her cousin, Amelia—both being granddaughters of John Fagan Everett—introduced their husbands to each other, and the result was that the Commodore donated $1 million to finance what became Vanderbilt University. What would have happened if the old widower had not been attracted to this cousin, a pretty Southern belle of thirty years of age? Would we still have that fine university? Anyway, Frank Crawford was also a second cousin twice removed to our grandfather, D. E. Coleman. Did he know this family history?

Joshua Everett

Joshua was born in Tyrrell County, North Carolina, in 1774 and moved with his parents, John and Sarah Everett, to Effingham County, Georgia, where they settled in that part of the county that was cut out to become Bulloch County. He married Jane, called "Jincy" Carter, in 1797 and had eleven children. The name of Jincy's parents has not been established although many of her descendants and some genealogists have researched and debated this matter for years; still no consensus. Joshua became one of the largest landowners in Bulloch County. In 1845, just a year before his death, he deeded about 7,000 acres of farm and timber lands to his children. The records show that he also owned some fifty slaves at that time.

Following in his father's footsteps, he participated in many civic activities. He served as a judge on the Bulloch County Inferior Court for two years beginning in 1819. On November 19, 1806, he was commissioned an ensign in the county militia and later in 1809 served as a captain in the 45th Militia District. He was a member of the Lower Lotts Creek Primitive Baptist Church.

He died at his home on Spring Creek in what is now Candler County and was buried in the Everett Cemetery on the old home place where his parents are also buried. After his death his widow moved to Thomas County, Georgia, and made her home with her son, Josiah, and his family as well as other family members in the area. She is buried in the Everett Cemetery just south of the small town of Boston in Thomas County.

Children of Joshua Everett and Jane "Jincy" Carter

1. Sarah C. b. Apr 7, 1799, d. Apr 14, 1876; m. Michael Young on Mar 25, 1876.

2. **John Carter, b. Sep 1, 1801; d. Nov 3, 1836; m. Elizabeth Ellis on Feb 22, 1824.**

3. William, b. Jan 24, 1804; died young.

4. Josiah J., b. Nov 10, 1806; d. Feb 26, 1873; m. Harriet Ann Archer on Jan 19, 1832.

5. Aaron Barber, b. Jun 20, 1809; d. unk; m. Sarah Tillman on Jan 28, 1836.

6. Cassandra, b. Sep 12, 1811; d. Oct 4, 1864; m. Joseph Isaiah Tillman on Jun 2, 1831.

7. Eliza Fagan, b. Nov 9, 1813; d. Mar 16, 1879; m. Benjamin Ellis on Feb 27, 1834.

8. Ann Jane, b. Jan 10, 1819; died young.

9. Joshua Bedford, b. Aug 1, 1818; d. Mar 10, 1875; m. Sarah Slater.

10. John (Jehu), b. Aug 10, 1822, d. Dec 10, 1906; m. Penelope Jones on Sep 5, 1844.

11. Pamelia, b. Sep 25, 1825; d. Jun 21, 1887; m. Hamilton H. Williams on Nov 30, 1848.

John Carter Everett

John C., Joshua Everett's oldest son, was born in Bulloch County in 1801. In 1824 he married Elizabeth, the daughter of Benjamin and Absolea Ellis, and they had six children before his early death curtailed more offspring. Records show that he was active in his community although not to the degree he probably would have been had he lived a normal life span. In 1824 he and his brother-in-law, Michael Young, were appointed to appraise the estate of Jacob Futch. He was named the executor of Philip Mincey's estate in 1825. In 1833 he was discharged from the securityship of the estate of John E. McCall.

The relationship between the Everett and Tillman families was, to say the least, close. John C.'s sister, Cassandra, was the second wife of Joseph Tillman. John C.'s two oldest sisters, Sarah and Susan, married the two Tillman brothers, James and Henry, the sons of the same Joseph Tillman by his first wife, Catherine. His other daughter, Margaret, married Jonathan Brewton, and their son, John Carter Brewton, was the founder and first president of Brewton-Parker College in Mt. Vernon, Georgia. John C.'s only son to survive to adulthood, John Carter, Jr., served as a sergeant in "D" Company, 61st Regiment of Georgia Infantry, and was killed on the first day of fighting at Gettysburg, leaving a wife and four children under the age of six.

Children of John Carter Everett and Elizabeth Ellis

1. **Sarah, b. Dec 5, 1824; d. Jul 18, 1898; m. James Tillman on Sep 3, 1840.**

2. Susan, b. May 5, 1826; d. 1845; m. Henry Tillman on Nov 22, 1843.

3. Josiah, b. Mar 5, 1828; d. May 1837.

4. Margaret, b. Oct 30, 1830; d. Apr. 9, 1919; m. Jonathan Brewton on Mar 30, 1848.

5. Missouri, b. Jun 5, 1834; died young.

6. John Carter, Jr., b. Feb. 28, 1839; d. Jul 1, 1863; m. Ann Jane Brennan on Jan 10, 1856. He was killed in the Civil War (see above).

The Holland Lineage

It is likely that the Hollands of Tattnall County, Georgia, are descended from John Holland who was among sixty people transported in 1664 from England to Nansemond County, Virginia, by Lt. Col. Blake and Edward Isom. John settled in this same county, where he accumulated some 1,700 acres of land. Little else is known about him except that he had six sons, one of whom was named Henry and who can be referred to as Henry (1) since there are many Henrys in the next few generations. Henry (1) is known principally because he shows up in deed books as a buyer and seller of land in Nansemond County. Henry (1) also had four sons including Henry (2) who died in 1789 and whose will was probated in Isle of Wight County, Virginia, a county which is located just to the southwest of Nansemond. Henry (2) had three sons, another Henry (3), Robert and Job. While it is not entirely clear, it is probably this Henry (3) who immigrated to Bertie County, North Carolina, and was the father of Henry (4) as described below. Also in Bertie County at this time was a man named Frederick Holland who was probably a brother of Henry (3).

Henry Holland

Henry Holland (4) was born on March 1, 1757, in Bertie County, the son of Henry Holland (3). Bertie County is just below the Virginia-North Carolina border and can be easily reached from southeastern Virginia by river or along the coast through Albemarle Sound. Henry (he doesn't have to be called (4) any more) served in the North Carolina militia during the Revolutionary War on three separate occasions, each time for three to six months. In each instance he served as a private in the Duplin County militia which county is located farther south in North Carolina and where he may have been living at the time.

In 1780 he enlisted for six months in Captain King's Company of Col. Kenan's Regiment and participated in the Battle of Stono, outside of Charleston, South Carolina, the battle having taken place in February 1781. Later in 1781 he joined up for three months, serving in Captain Tool's Company of Col. Brown's Regiment. After that hitch was completed he enlisted once again in 1781 for six months, this time in Captain Benjamin Coleman's Company of Col. Murphy's Regiment. He fought in the Battle of Eutaw Springs, which took place in District 96 in northwest South Carolina. Although hard fought, with hand-to-hand combat and heavy casualties, the Americans should have won that battle. Col. Wade Hampton distinguished himself for his bravery in this battle while Col. Francis Marion showed that his militia troops could stand up well against British regulars. But, on the verge of victory, the Continentals and militia found themselves amid untold riches in the British camp and went wild in an orgy of drunken looting. This gave the British time to regroup and to expel the Americans from the field.

As a result of his Revolutionary War service, Henry was authorized a pension on May 6, 1833. On June 26, 1853, his widow applied for a pension for his military service during the war, and it was granted. The information regarding Henry's war service is contained in these pension applications.

In the same year that the peace treaty ending the war was signed, Henry married Sarah Clay; that was on September 2, 1783. About five years later they moved to Warren County, Georgia, and then in 1799 to Washington County, Georgia, where he settled in the part of the county that was later cut out to form Tattnall County. In 1804 he received two-hundred acres of bounty land in Montgomery County, Georgia, and later in 1812, another two-hundred acres along Wolf Creek in Tattnall County. In 1815 and again in 1818 Henry was on the Tattnall County list of Grand Jurors. He built a home on his farm located on the west bank of the Canoochee River.

Henry laid out a cemetery ground on his property on a hill overlooking the river. Today the Henry Holland Cemetery can be found on State Highway 129 between Metter and Claxton, Georgia. However, there are only a few tombstones or markers still there. The DAR erected markers to Henry and to two of his grandsons, Thomas Holland and John B. Holland, who fought in the Civil War. Nevertheless Henry, who died on June 2, 1852, and his wife, Sarah, are almost certainly buried here.

Children of Henry Holland and Sarah Clay

1. David, b. 1784; d. between 1850 and 1860; m. Pricilla Hollingworth on Dec 25, 1814.

2. John, b. 1785; d. between 1860 and 1870; m. Rachel Collins on Jul 8, 1827.

3. Dempsey, b. 1791; d. Dec 31, 1852; m. Jane Howard on Jan 8, 1815.

4. William, b. 1793; d. unk; m. Polly Ann White.

5. **Frederick, b. 1794; d. Jun 6, 1881; m. Matilda Lewis on Jul 6, 1820.**

6. Elizabeth, b. 1797; d. unk; m. Miel Collins.

7. Mary, b. 1798; d. after 1836; m. Stephen Kennedy.

8. Sarah, b. 1803; d. unk; m. William K. Collins.

9. James, b. 1805; d. 1839; m. Martha Underwood on Mar 11, 1827.

Frederick Holland

Frederick was born in 1794 in Washington County, Georgia, in the part of the county that became Tattnall County nine years later. His parents were Henry and Sarah Clay Holland. Frederick married Matilda Lewis in 1820, and they settled on a farm at the headwaters of Cedar Creek near present day Cobbtown, Georgia. Matilda was the daughter of George and Cynthia Lewis of whom little is known except that Matilda was one of their five siblings, the others being Nancy, Stephen, Hanson and Smith. Nancy may have had some physical or mental problems because she is identified in court records as a pauper and is shown living at various times with relatives in the Coleman and Holland families who were paid by the county to maintain her.

Frederick acquired several pieces of property in the Cedar Creek area through land grants under the headright law. In June

1836 he was deeded 360 acres next to Joseph Tillman's property and then in July 1837 he obtained another 310 acres just next to the earlier purchased property. He had probably settled on this land in earlier years and had only been able to survey and legalize his ownership in these later years. In 1858 he obtained another 116 acres to round out his land holdings. In all likelihood he harvested timber on his property for sale down river and, of course, he farmed along the banks of Cedar Creek. In the 1860 census, his real estate was valued at $500 while his other assets totaled $1,500.

He hardly ever appears in the county or state records although this might be an oversight. One instance he appears is when the court paid him $5 to maintain Nancy Lewis, pauper. Obviously he lived a quiet life in the woods while raising a large family. Another interest of his may have been his church. Frederick and Matilda were members of the Cedar Creek Primitive Baptist Church. He was among the first deacons of the reorganized Cedar Creek-Mount Horeb Church. In 1854 he deeded over to this church the 116 acres that four years later he recorded to legalize this transfer. Actually he deeded the property to himself and J. Solomon Kennedy as deacons of the church and to their successors in office at the same church. The deed stipulated that the land would be held in trust for the Cedar Creek Church for so long as it remained a place of worship. The church continues to have the privileges and use of this land today.

Children of Frederick Holland and Matilda Lewis

1. Dempsey, b. 1821; d. between 1860 and 1870; m. Martha Anderson on Feb 20, 1840.

2. Willoughby Berrien, b. Oct 24, 1822; d. Oct 24, 1902; m. Ellender Yeomans.

3. **Elizabeth, b. Mar 13, 1825; d. Nov 17, 1895; m. Jeremiah Coleman on Jan 2, 1850.**

4. Lewis, b. 1828; d. 1862; m. 1st Sarah Ann Yeomans on Mar 26, 1848, 2nd Caroline Sapp on Dec 31, 1849.

5. Martha, b. Dec 9, 1832; d. Apr 3, 1908; m. Eli Coleman, date unk. Eli was the brother of Jeremiah Coleman who married her sister, Elizabeth.

6. Nancy Ann, b. 1835; d. Apr 7, 1911; m. Clement T. Bowen on May 3, 1868.

7. David Henry; b. Mar 3, 1837; d. Aug 21, 1920; m. 1st Dica Kennedy on Nov 15, 1855, 2nd Sarah Ann Boyett on Oct 25, 1860.

8. Polly Ann, b. Jun 12, 1839; d. Mar 2, 1895; m. John L. Lynn on Oct 28, 1858.

9. Matilda, b. 1842; d. 1895; m. Thomas Boyett on Aug. 10, 1865

Chapter 2

Between the Rivers
The Hargrove Family

Family Tree for
Alice Viola Hargrove: Between the Rivers
4 Generations

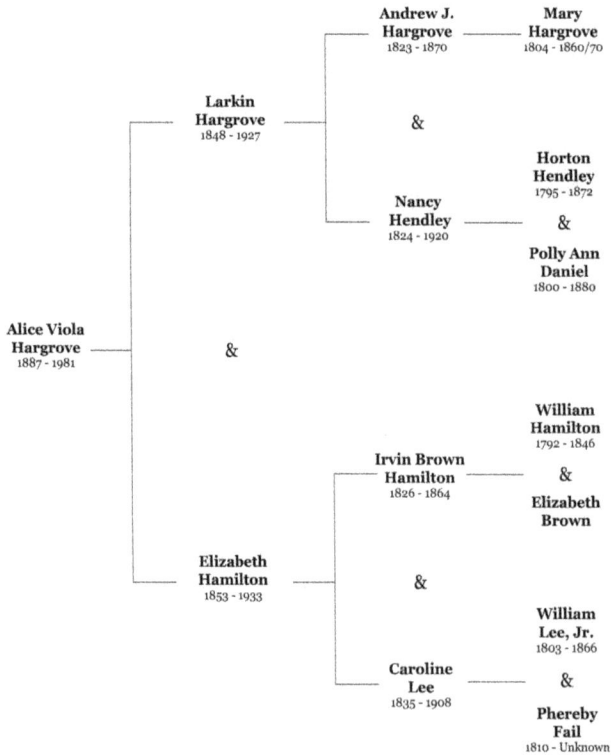

Andrew J.
Hargrove ———— Mary
1823 - 1870 Hargrove
1804 - 1860/70

Larkin
Hargrove ————
1848 - 1927

&

Horton
Hendley
1795 - 1872

Nancy
Hendley ————— &
1824 - 1920

Polly Ann
Daniel
1800 - 1880

Alice Viola
Hargrove ————
1887 - 1981

&

William
Hamilton
1792 - 1846

Irvin Brown
Hamilton ————— &
1826 - 1864

Elizabeth
Brown

Elizabeth
Hamilton —————
1853 - 1933

&

William
Lee, Jr.
1803 - 1866

Caroline
Lee ————— &
1835 - 1908

Phereby
Fail
1810 - Unknown

Chapter 2

Between the Rivers
The Hargrove Family

The Hargrove family tree consists of four families who settled in the early part of the nineteenth century in that part of middle Georgia comprising mainly Pulaski and Dodge Counties. The principal family here is the Hargrove family although the origin of this family was, and still is, essentially unknown until the appearance of Andrew Jackson Hargrove, born in 1823, even though it is likely that we can trace his lineage back to an emigrant ancestor. The other families—Hamilton, Hendley and Lee—can be documented further back for several generations, mostly to North

Carolina and Virginia/Maryland before they moved directly to Georgia. This area of middle Georgia is located between two important river basins, the Oconee and Ocmulgee, both of which were crucial to the region's development, hence the name given to this chapter.

The Hargrove Lineage

The first Hargrove in our line to arrive in the New World was Richard Hargrove, who came to Virginia on the ship *Bonaventure* in 1634 as an indentured servant. After completing his service commitment in Norfolk he remained in that area, married Mary Bray, although it is not certain if this was her maiden name, had several children, and became a successful and well-respected member of his community. The *Hargrove Family Study*, a genealogical study of Richard's descendants, traces the Richard Hargrove family line that has spread throughout the southeastern states, including middle Georgia. The author has drawn a very clear linkage between Richard on the one hand and a large group of Hargroves from Duplin County, North Carolina, on the other hand, who arrived in Washington County, Georgia, (later Montgomery County) in the 1790s. These Hargroves were named Hardy, Jordan, Jacob, Randall, Reuben, Josiah and Howell. It is highly likely that one of these men was the father of Andrew Jackson Hargrove, but no proof yet.

Andrew Jackson Hargrove

The origins of Andrew Jackson Hargrove, called Jackson all his life, have been the subject of much debate and discussion. That he was the son of Mary, or Molsey, Hargrove and was born on September 26, 1823, in Montgomery County has never been seriously in doubt. In 1825 Mary Hargrove, a widow living in Montgomery County, was declared eligible for the Land Lottery that year. Thus we know that two years after the birth of her son, Jackson, she was a widow, her surname was Hargrove and she lived in the county. However, two years later—and this is the issue—records show one of the applicants in the 1827 Land Lottery was "A. J. Hargrove, ill. McMillon [a military district] no. 38, Dt. 15, Sec. 5. Montgomery County". The four year old applicant, obviously young Jackson Hargrove, was awarded some land, but the application states clearly that he was illegitimate. That is what "ill" means.

Fortunately, DNA testing has proved that a Hargrove was Jackson's father, but that does not tell us which Hargrove was his father, nor does it mean that Mary was married to a Hargrove even though she gave Hargrove as her surname. There are no records showing she had been married, although that does not necessarily mean she never married. On the other hand, why would she have stated that her son was illegitimate if he was not so born that way? Yet there are reasons, one being that illegitimate children were treated as orphans and were given two draws in the lottery rather than the usual opportunity of one person one draw. After all, she was a young twenty four year old mother with a four year old child but no husband. My belief is that we will probably never know who his father was.

Despite all this information about Jackson's origins, we still do not know Mary Hargrove's maiden name, unless, of course, it was Hargrove as well, although the odds of that being the case are not good. In 1827 Mary married Peter McEachin, an immigrant from Scotland who had first settled in Robeson County, North Carolina, where there was a large Scottish community, before moving to Georgia. The same year that Peter and Mary married, the courts recognized Peter as Jackson's legal guardian. Jackson was raised in the McEachin home along with the seven children born to Peter and Mary. Given Peter's place of birth it is said that Jackson always spoke with a slight accent and used some Scottish words and phrases as did all of Peter's children.

Jackson and, later, his children, retained an association with their Robeson County relations. His descendants recalled being told that he was a surveyor from Robeson County who came to Pulaski County to work, along with a brother who moved later to Texas. How much of that is true is debatable but if it is so then he might have lived for a while in Robeson County, where he learned surveying and then moved back to Pulaski. At some point he became a boarder in the home of Horton Hendley where he met and married Nancy Hendley, Horton's daughter, on September 28, 1843. He was twenty and she nineteen. Incidentally three of Jackson's children, William, Annie and James, found their spouses in Robeson County.

Jackson turned to farming for a living, as most men did in Pulaski County. His farm was located a few miles south of where Eastman would later be founded, at a place near Sugar Creek that became known as Hargrove Crossing. In his will he left to his wife parts of land sections 28 and 25 in the 15th District of Pulaski

County, totaling 303.75 acres. Together with his home and farm buildings this appears to be all the property he owned. Their home was a classic example of rural homes in the South at that time. It began as a single room or what was called a "one log pen," but when Jackson added two rooms across the open hall, it was known as a "double log pen house." This house configuration is sometimes referred to as a "dogtrot." Photographs of this log house still exist, which is fortunate since part of it was dismantled and moved many years later to the property of Audrey Hargrove Cofield, who is Jackson's great grand-daughter. What remains of this house can be seen on her property.

Throughout his life Jackson was an active member of the Baptist church. In 1855 he was elected clerk of the Parkerson Primitive Baptist Church, the church in which he was baptized and which was close to his home. In 1862 he acted as church moderator and then, on the second Sunday of June 1864, he was ordained to preach at his church, a position he continued until his death. By all accounts Jackson, if he was born illegitimate, overcame the handicap of his birth (if known then) and became one of the most respected and well-loved men in his community.

In the summer of 1864 when Sherman's army was rampaging through Georgia, Jackson, the Baptist minister, wrote a letter to Irvin B. Hamilton, a close friend and congregant, whose daughter Elizabeth would, after Jackson's death, marry Jackson's son Larkin. At that time Irvin had been sent to Atlanta to reinforce the Confederate Army's defense of the city. But a sick Irvin had been evacuated from Atlanta to a Macon hospital where he died of dysentery a few weeks later. The letter copied in the nearby box was found in his possession afterwards and was preserved by the family. It is not known whether Irvin, who may well have known that his time was short, was cheered up by this letter or not. It is presented intact although some assumptions have been made about certain unreadable words which are shown in brackets. Some punctuation may have been added but the misspellings were not changed. The grammatical errors are his as well.

Andrew J. Hargrove letter to Irvin B. Hamilton

Georgia, Pulaski Co July 21, 1864

Dear Friend

I resumed my seat to drop you a few lines which inform you that we are all well at this time. Truly hope this may come to hand and find you enjoying the same. I. B., I have not [wanted] to write you that times seem to get no better but worse every day. We had nothing here but women and children. Now the children has to leave, [none left] but women and the little ones. What a community is ours, not a [man] to bury the dead, hardly. You people is all and doing well. I.B., I wish I had some interesting news to write you to cheer your feelings. But I will [tell] you this much of an old thing. Remember you are a dying man. The time is short, years at most when you like myself must pass away. Christ says ye must be born again. I.B., procrastination is the thief of time. Time rolls on and waits for none. Be ye ready. By the help of God make the preparation. What a solemn thought is Death. I send you this little epistle to let you know that I have not forgotten you [and] well wishes your soul. I hope you will take this truth and put it into execution. Now is the time. Today is the day of salvation. Perhaps your chance is a bad one but the Lord has promised to hear them that cry unto him. If the Lord is for you what can be against you, so watch and pray, see the Lord while he may be found and call on him while he is near, I.B., will you take this admonition or will you not. Yours as ever. Write soon.   A. J. Hargrove

---

Jackson's only participation during the Civil War was as a private in the District 349 Militia Company in Pulaski County that was commanded by his friend, Irvin B. Hamilton. By the time his son, Larkin, was conscripted into the Army in 1864 he was an ordained minister which probably exempted him from military service. He was also forty one years old that year and would live only six more years, dying on September 27, 1870.

Jackson's wife Nancy survived him by almost fifty years. Two of her sons, Levi and Thomas, never married and lived with her the rest of her life. On her birthday in 1920 the UDC, at her home and in the presence of some two-hundred people, presented to her the Confederate Bar of Honor "in recognition of the most sacred gift that could be made by a patriotic woman." She was ninety six on that day and was being recognized as the mother of a living Confederate veteran, her son Larkin, who had enlisted in the army at the age of sixteen. Nancy was only the sixth living Confederate mother so honored in Georgia and the twenty sixth in the United States.

An article in the *Eastman Times Journal* on that July day tells a lot about Nancy's life. "She was married at the age of nineteen to Andrew Jackson Hargrove, a minister of the gospel, and to them was born eleven children, nine of whom are still living. The eldest of these children is 76 and the youngest is 52 years of age. Her immediate family consists of 161 members, viz: nine children, 55 grandchildren, 85 great-grandchildren and 12 great-great grandchildren. Two of her sons are great-grandfathers and her only daughter is a great-grandmother. Mrs. Hargrove resides at the same home to which she moved 65 years ago and which is within five or six miles of where she was born and reared. She is a remarkable woman in that, despite her 96 years, she can still get about and perform little household tasks that seem almost impossible for someone of her years. She has a bright, clear mind and can readily recall many incidents of the sixties. She also keeps abreast of the times and can discuss current events as intelligently as anyone."

She died on July 15, 1920, a few months after this ceremony. One of her great-grandchildren, Louise Hargrove Webb, wrote to someone many years later about the funeral. "They had her funeral at Parkerson [Church] but before that she was at home in her coffin. The furniture was moved out of that room. At Parkerson, her sons, all grey bearded, and Aunt Jane [Hargrove Brown] sat in the front pew. I don't remember her dress but the sheerest pale pink scarf was tied loosely around her head and under her chin. Her face was as smooth as baby skin and she was still tiny and pretty at 96."

Jackson and Nancy are buried at Parkerson Baptist Church cemetery, the church of his ministry, which is located by traveling south from Eastman on Highway 341 for about three miles, then turning left on country road 251 for 2.5 miles to the church. There is also a large marker in front of the church indicating that Jackson had been a minister of this church, but it incorrectly states that he was the first minister; he was not. While Jackson's headstone is in this graveyard, it is claimed that, in actuality, he was buried in the Harrell family cemetery which is about three miles from the church on the McCranie farm and later removed to this cemetery. Many of Jackson and Nancy's children are buried in the Parkerson Church cemetery.

Children of Andrew Jackson Hargrove and Nancy Hendley

1. Jane Ann, b. Jul 8, 1844; d. Oct 1, 1928; m. Jordan Brown.

2. Horton, died early.

3. **Larkin Llmore., b. Mar 21, 1848; d. Feb 20, 1927; m. Elizabeth Hamilton on Nov 23, 1871.**

4. Perry S., b. Feb 8, 1851; d. Oct 29, 1924; m. Subriney M. Nicholson on Jul 28, 1870.

5. Andrew J. Jr., b. 1852; d. Jan 22, 1928; m. Jennie McCranie on Mar 16, 1876.

6. John Hendley, b. Oct 12, 1856; d. Sep 11, 1924; m. Mary Virginia McRae on Dec 19, 1877.

7. William D., b. Feb 12, 1859; d. Feb 24, 1937; m. Lydia Wishart on Sep 18, 1886.

8. Annie, b. 1861; d. unk; m. R. E. Wishart on Apr 2, 1879.

9. Thomas Hendley (Hen), b. Jun 4, 1863; d. Jul 1, 1826; never married.

10. Levi F (Leve), b. 1864; d. 1940; never married.

11. James Franklin, b. Jan 7, 1868; d. Mar 9, 1951; m. Annie Rowland on Apr 22, 1891.

Larkin Llmore Hargrove

Larkin, or rather just Lark, Hargrove was the oldest son of Jackson and Nancy Hargrove. His unusual middle name, Llmore, may have been derived from an ancestor of his father's stepfather who was born and reared in Scotland, although it could be Welsh as well. One of the memorable events his life, if not the most, occurred when he was conscripted into the army in July of 1864 and served as a private in "F" Company, 7th Regiment of Georgia Militia. The story is that when the county officials came to the farm to muster him into the army on the day he turned sixteen his mother convinced them to let him stay on the farm a little while longer until the seeds were planted, after which she would let him go. She kept her word and in a short time off he went.

Lark's unit was ordered to help defend Atlanta. When the battle began in earnest in mid-July of 1864, Lark had arrived just in time to find himself in the very midst of the fighting. His regiment was one of three assigned to the 3rd Brigade, commanded by Brig. Gen. Charles D. Anderson. In turn the 3rd Brigade was one of four in the 1st Division of Georgia Militia under the command of Maj. Gen. Gustavus W. Smith. The commander of 7th Regiment, Lark's unit, was Col. Abner Redding.

Battle maps show that the 1st Division was posted to the northeast sector of Atlanta's defenses, covering the defensive line from Peachtree Road in the north to Auburn Avenue in the east. At one time during the battle Lark reported that he was posted to a position beside a two-story brick house which is depicted today at the Cyclorama in Atlanta. After this famous battle scene was constructed, Lark and a longtime friend, Judge C. B. Murrell of Eastman, who had fought with him there, would make periodic pilgrimages to view that battle scene and give thanks for having survived the war.

After Atlanta fell at the end of August 1864, the 1st Division retired further southward while Gen. Sherman prepared his army for the march to Savannah and the sea. When the march began, Gen. Thomas, who commanded the Union Army's right wing, pushed toward Macon and reported that "I found some resistance from Gen. G. W. Smith's new levies. The crossing of the Ocmulgee, with its steep and muddy banks was hard enough for the [wagon] trains. . .Smith crossed the river and gave us battle at Griswoldville [just east of Macon]. . .Smith was badly defeated. . ." This was on November 22, 1864.

The Battle of Griswoldville was the largest battle fought between the two armies during Sherman's march to the sea. Once the battle began, the 3rd Brigade advanced on the Union's dug-in positions. A Union major reported that "as soon as they [the Georgia militia] came within range, a most terrific fire was poured into their ranks, doing fearful execution. . .still they moved forward and came within 45 yards of our works. Here they attempted to reform their line, but so destructive was the fire that they were compelled to retire." The Confederates reported 51 killed and 422 wounded, and among those killed was Col. Abner Redding, the commander of the 7th Regiment, Lark's regiment. It is highly likely that Lark was among those charging the Union lines. Lark was truly fortunate to have survived this battle.

Gen. Smith then withdrew his 1st Division from the Macon area and "moved by rail to Albany, thence across the country [on foot] to Thomasville, and from the latter point by rail to Savannah." The troop train had to pass through Valdosta to reach Savannah, allowing Lark the first opportunity to see the town where, many years later, his daughter, Alice, would make her home. Because of a lack of railroad stock, the division arrived piecemeal in Savannah in late November and early December of 1864.

After Savannah was lost and the city evacuated, the 1st Division was ordered to Augusta to protect that city and its valuable gun powder works from Union Army raids. It is probable that when the South, at long last, gave up that gallant struggle, the division, with its 3rd Brigade, was posted to the capital city of Milledgeville, where it, with Lark, surrendered in April, 1865. In a nine month period, Lark had gone through enough experiences for a lifetime. He then went home.

In 1871 Lark married Elizabeth Hamilton, who had been living with her mother and four siblings on a farm not far from the Hargrove home place in what is now Dodge County. Her father, Irvin B. Hamilton, had died in the war when she was just nine years old. Larkin and Lizziebeth, as he called her, had ten children. Lark had a large farm where he mainly grew cotton. He also had a commercial cotton gin for his own cotton as well as to gin that of others. He built a home in Eastman, although he kept his country home which he used frequently during the farming season.

To support his cotton farming interests, he became a member of the Farmer's Union and in 1907 was named a director of the Dodge County branch. Lark combined farming with a number of business interests in Eastman. Those interests included a part ownership and directorship in a local Dodge County bank. When the bank failed during the Panic of 1896, he and other owners paid off all the depositors with their own money, estimated at $90,000, a considerable sum in those days. Bankruptcy was not a valid option in a small town where everyone knew everyone else.

Among other activities he was a member of Masonic Lodge 279 in Eastman. When Dodge County was created out of Pulaski County in 1870 he served on the first grand jury, and, throughout his life, his name appeared frequently as one of the those citizens who served on various juries. He was also appointed in October

1891 to a county committee whose purpose was to try to bring another railroad through the county.

Letters and reminiscences indicate that Lark and Lizziebeth's home was a warm and happy one. Christmas at Grandma's house was a very special event, as described by their granddaughter Louise: "We always went to Grandma and Grandpa Hargrove's on Christmas—for many years in a buggy. This was in 1907. All the family came. It was fun going through the creek at the bottom of the hill at Mullentown. Sometimes the water was swift and would come on the floorboards. Grandpa would have a crate of oranges, a barrel of apples, cartons of raisins and many cartons of candy. Dinner was chicken and all kinds of fresh pork ham, pickled peaches, cake and a stack of sweet potato pies. Wonderful to remember. They managed all that crowd as if it was easy. I know now it wasn't. There was a tree in the parlor and presents for each one of us."

Lark's obituary said that he had died at 11:35 am on Sunday, February 20, 1927, "following a long illness of paralysis [stroke], he having been an invalid for the past two years". His widow lived until 1933, dying at the age of eighty. They are buried at the Parkerson Baptist Church, with other family members.

Children of Larkin Llmore Hargrove and Elizabeth Hamilton

1. William Jackson, b. Aug 9, 1872; d, Dec 16, 1909. He was a twin brother to John Irvin. He never married and apparently suffered from what today sounds like severe depression, dying at his parents' house at the age of thirty seven.

2. John Irvin, b. Aug 9, 1872; d. May 6, 1942; m. Hattie Eugenia Clark on Jun 6, 1897. He was a farmer and businessman, and the family lived for some years in the Forsyth House near Chauncey. In the 1930s they moved to Tampa. Their daughter Dorothy Hargrove Stoeger, who now lives near Kansas City, Missouri, has kept the Hargrove family's history alive.

3. Augustus B., b. Jan 16, 1875; d. Jun 1961; m. Cassie Geroma (Romie) Clark on Dec 24, 1900.

4. Mary (Dosia), b. Nov 25, 1877; d. May 13, 1952; m. 1st George S. Offerman on Feb 19, 1900, and 2nd Thomas J. Montford.

5. Annie Bell, b. Jul 19, 1879; d. Jun 26, 1942; m. John Thomas Rogers on May 1904.

6. Charles Bartlett, b. Nov 15, 1882; d. June 1, 1964; m. Bertie Kent Livingston on Sep 30, 1916. He stayed in Dodge County to farm. His daughter, Audrey, married Ellis Cofield, and it is on their place that the old Jackson Hargrove home now sits. Her daughter, Carol married Terry Coleman, and there is always the thought that he might be related to the Colemans of Tattnall County. No proof yet.

7. **Alice Viola, b. Feb 24, 1887; d. Jun 6, 1981; m. Daniel Ernest Coleman on Dec 24, 1906.** Alice moved to Valdosta with her husband and is the grandmother of the author of this family history.

8. Levi Lewis, b. Apr 30, 1889; d. Jan 30, 1960; m. Lessie J. Graham, Apr 21, 1918.

9. Minnie Jane, b. May 6, 1893; d. Jul 7, 1968; m. William Walter Parkerson on Nov 12, 1922.

10. Larkin Milton, b. Jan 30, 1895; d. Jun 18, 1926; never married. Milton joined the U. S. Infantry when he was 23 and was

sent to France during WWI where he was gassed. When he returned he never seemed to be able to find his niche in life. He never married but it is believed that the baby who was left at his parent's was Milton's daughter. The child was reared by Lark and Elizabeth as one of the family. A notice in the Eastman newspaper reported that Milton died at Allen's Sanitarium, Milledgeville, following an illness of several weeks. He was thirty one.

The Hamilton Lineage

The first documented Hamilton in this line is a William Hamilton whose date of birth is unknown but who died in about 1786. He moved with his family to the area of North Carolina that encompasses the counties of Chowan and Tyrrell. Some genealogists have written that he was descended from a John Hamilton of Nansemond County, Virginia. Most have rejected that claim, so if anyone reads about this John Hamilton being the first in our line, take it with a grain of salt.

William left a will in Wake County, North Carolina, where he had settled, although some parts of the will are unclear as to whom or even if he was, in fact, married. His will leaves to his daughter, "Kesiah Dorman alias Hamilton, who was esteemed my legitimate daughter though I never was married to her mother. . ." The will then goes on saying, "I give and bequeath to Andrew and Stewart [his sons]. . .the children of said Rachel Dorman who go by the name of Hamilton. . ." No other woman is mentioned although several other children are, all with the same disclaimer. Was she simply his common-law wife, or a wife that he had stopped living with and wanted to forget? Or was he trying from the legal standpoint to exclude her from his inheritance? Other researchers and genealogists have raised the possibility that she may have been an Indian or part Indian, and because it was illegal for mixed Indian/white marriages to take place, such statements as these would help make sure that his children would not be disinherited by the authorities. One respected genealogist believes that William was a member of a religious sect that believed in polygamy. Regardless of its importance the most interesting part of all this, from the genealogical standpoint, is that he identified his son, Stewart, as the next person in our line.

Stewart Hamilton

Stewart was born in 1760 into this "dysfunctional" family. He moved with his parents from the place of his birth, Tyrrell County, North Carolina, to Wake County, probably sometime in the 1770s. His father, William, and Stewart had recorded land deeds in 1779 in Wake County. On May 25, 1781, Stewart joined the Continental Army in North Carolina for one year serving in Capt. Benjamin Bailey's Company of the 1th Regiment. This company was serving as a part of the 3rd Regiment when Stewart was discharged. The unit fought at the Battle of Eutaw Springs, the same battle in which George Holland (see Chapter 1) was a participant.

Stewart married Clarissa Stringer, born in Edgecombe County, North Carolina, in about 1780/81. One report gives her father as a William Stringer but nothing else. In the 1790 Census of North Carolina, Stewart and his family were recorded in the Hillsborough District, Wake County, where most of his children were born. In about 1802 they relocated to Montgomery County, Georgia, acquiring land on what is today Braddy Road. By 1805 Stewart was paying taxes in Montgomery. He also had a draw from that county in the 1805 Land Lottery, and in 1807 he received a grant of two-hundred acres. He continued to acquire land which he left to his wife when he died.

He established a burial ground near his home which is still known as the Hamilton or Hamilton Hill Cemetery and where Stewart and Clarissa and many of their descendants are buried. In 1915 the William Few chapter of the DAR marked his grave with military honors. Two ladies from the DAR were present for the unveiling of a tombstone, noting his military service in the Revolutionary War. A large dinner was spread down from the hill in front of the cemetery and many descendants were present.

To reach the cemetery, drive north for about 4 miles on Georgia Hwy 15 from the intersection of 15 and 292. Turn left on Braddy Road and go about a mile. The cemetery is in a field on the left, about 100 yards from the road; it can be seen from there.

Children of Stewart Hamilton and Clarissa Stringer

1. **William, b. 1772; d. Jul 26, 1846; m. Elizabeth Brown.**

2. Benjamin, b. 1774; d. unk; m. Miss Walker.

3. John, b. 1789; d. 1856, m. Margaret Cadwell in 1810.

4. Sarah, b. Feb. 15, 1790; d. Aug 15, 1871; m. Benjamin Burch on Jul 26, 1814.

5. Rebecca, b. unk; d. unk; m. Samuel Story.

6. Josiah, b. May, 1794; d. Apr 22, 1869; m. 1st Mary Poole and 2nd Mary Wiggins Darley.

7. Rosanna, b. 1797, d. unk; m. 1st James Calhoun on Sep 3, 1812 and 2nd John Gillis in Aug 1840.

8. Solomon, b. unk; d. unk; m. Stephen Grimes on Feb 20, 1828.

9. Clarissa, b. 1802; d. 1850; m. John Connell on Jul 10, 1824.

10. Cynthia, b. unk; d. unk; never married.

William Hamilton

William was the oldest son of Stewart Hamilton. Born in 1782 in North Carolina, he moved with his father to Montgomery County, Georgia. There he married Elizabeth Brown, who was probably the daughter of Benjamin Brown, an early settler in the area who lived close to the Hamilton holdings. As noted below in the list of William and Elizabeth's children, their oldest son was named Benjamin Brown and many of his other sons carried the middle name of Brown.

As Georgia expanded westward William Hamilton moved into the vacant lands, the Indians having been pushed even farther west, and settled in the area soon to be known as Pulaski County. He surveyed some land on the east side of the Ocmulgee River and began to expand his holdings along Sugar Creek almost to the river. William served as the captain of the 349th Military District in Pulaski County in 1822. He also represented the county in the Georgia State Legislature from 1841 to 1843. His will was probated on July 25, 1846, in Pulaski County, and it indicated that he was a pretty well-to-do person. In it he gives the names of all his children but, more interestingly, he gives the names of all thirty two of his slaves.

He died at the age of sixty four in 1846. He and Elizabeth were buried in the Hamilton Family cemetery on their property. However, that cemetery was completely destroyed in the late 1960s or early 1970s by a timber logging company, who plowed over it. No records of the persons buried there were saved; thus we do not know anything more comprehensive about many dates of birth and death. We do know William's date of death because there was a law suit filed which protested his will. In it was his exact date of death.

Children of William Hamilton and Elizabeth Brown

1. Benjamin Brown, b. Jan 29, 1811; d. Feb 14, 1875; m. Laura Ann Jones. He moved to Dooly County and built his home in an area that later became the town of Cordele in Crisp County. Early on, he blazed that part of the state road in Dooly County that ran from Macon to Troupville in Lowndes County. He was a state representative from his county and also served as a judge on the inferior court. During the Civil War he served Georgia Gov. Brown as an Aide de Camp, and according to a letter Benjamin wrote to him which is in the State Archives, he appeared to focus on recruitment issues. He also sheltered Gov. Brown at his home when the latter fled Milledgeville in 1864.

2. Bartlett, no information but probably born in 1813. He was still in Pulaski County when he witnessed a deed in February 1847.

3. James Milton, b. Jan 16, 1815; d. Jun 28, 1881; m. Mary Susannah Whitehead on Nov 15, 1859.

4. William G., b. Mar 23, 1818; d. Oct 15, 1879; m. Mary Ann Burch on Jul 14, 1848.

5. John Jackson, b. Mar 25, 1820; d. Jun 9, 1882; m. Margaret Daniel on May 14, 1848.

6. Elizabeth Ann, b. Dec 23, 1822; d. Oct 17, 1879; m. Lovard L. Harrell on Jan 11, 1838.

7. Sarah Elizabeth, b. Apr 13, 1824; d. Oct 6, 1898; m. Wright W. Harrell on Sep 9, 1839.

8. **Irvin Brown, b. Jan 31, 1826; d. Aug 6, 1864; m. Caroline Lee on Dec 28, 1849.**

9. Ashley B., b. 1827; d. unk; m. 1st Pauline D. Outlaw on Jun 1, 1852 and 2nd Narcissa Staley on Jan 14, 1858. He relocated to Jackson County, Florida, in the late 1850's. During the Civil War he was the captain of a company called the Black Hawk Cavalry in the 1st Brigade, Florida Volunteer Militia. This unit was demobilized after six months, and no further mention is made of him during the war.

10. Warren B., b. Jan 23, 1833; d. Sep 29, 1881; m. Caldonia Baskin on Jan 1, 1857.

11. Catherine, b. 1839, d. unk; m. John Harrell on Nov 4, 1858.

Irvin Brown Hamilton

Irvin, sometimes called I. B., was born in Pulaski County, Georgia, in 1826. He was still a minor, by one year, when his father died, and Irvin's oldest brother, Benjamin, was made his legal guardian. He was the only one of all his brothers who remained on the family's estate near Sugar Creek in what is now Dodge County. His father had owned a large estate stretching from the creek to the Ocmulgee River which he left to his wife and children. Irvin inherited some of this land, but he may have used his share of the estate proceeds to buy land from his brothers as they resettled in other places. Dorothy Hargrove Stoeger, his granddaughter, remembered seeing a portrait of Irvin in the front hall of Larkin Hargrove's home and describes him as a handsome and distinguished looking young man with shoulder-length hair. When he was twenty three he married Caroline Lee, who was only fourteen at the time. Caroline was the daughter of William Lee, a pioneer settler in the region.

The 1860 Census shows that the value of Irvin's assets was $1,000 in real property and $13,900 in other assets which consisted mainly of the value of his twelve slaves, six of whom were adults. At the beginning of the Civil War, slave owning planters like Irvin were allowed an exemption of one white male for every twenty slaves on his plantation. Since Irvin had only twelve slaves in 1860, this exemption would not apply to him unless he had acquired additional slaves or borrowed more from other planters in the following years. Regardless, the Georgia State Legislature abolished all exemptions and substitutions in the winter of 1863-64 and made all healthy white males between the ages of seventeen and fifty eligible for the military service.

Early on in the war Irvin was appointed a captain in the county militia, District 349. As the military manpower needs increased, he was mustered into the Georgia Home Guards as a lieutenant of 1st Company in the 14th Military District under Major John J. Lee. This unit was reconstituted as "F" Company, 22nd Regiment of Georgia Cavalry. On May 27, 1864, Irvin was sworn in as a member in this unit and sent to Atlanta to take part in the defense of that city. That regiment may have been converted into infantry and renamed the 7th Regiment of Infantry since that was his unit when he died. The frequent reorganizations and unit consolidations during that time, resulting from declines in manpower and hasty deployment of replacement troops and units, coupled with lost records, has left much confusion about who was in which unit and when.

Prior to this deployment the Georgia State Home Guards were organized into a Division commanded by Gen. Gustavus Smith, a West Pointer somewhat past his prime. Its soldiers consisted of state militia troops and civil officers, many of whom were young boys of sixteen or seventeen (like Larkin Hargrove) or older men. This Division was under the direct control of Georgia's Gov. Joseph Brown, not the Confederate government. At its peak it never exceeded five thousand effectives and more often had as few as two thousand.

In a report dated September 15, 1864, Gen. Smith describes his command during the Battle of Atlanta in this way. "The militia, although poorly armed, very few having proper equipments, more than two-thirds of them without cartridge boxes, almost without ambulances or other transportation, most of the reserves never having been drilled at all, and the others but a few days, all performed well every service required of them during an arduous and dangerous campaign. They have been in service about one hundred days, during at least fifty of which they have been under close fire of the enemy mostly night and day. They have done good and substantial service in the cause of their country, and have established the fact that Georgia is willing and able to do something effective in her own name." Yet they fought on, along with the regular troops, outnumbered and under supplied, until, at last they abandoned Atlanta at the end of August 1864. Irvin would never live to see that loss and that retreat.

Military exertions under the conditions described above are bound to bring on health problems and while Irvin was a relatively young man of thirty eight years of age, something may have been physically wrong. This is probably why he wanted to limit his time in the service. On June 1, 1864, shortly after he had arrived in Atlanta, he wrote his wife a letter. Given its age this letter is very difficult to read, and in some places, it is guess work as to what exactly he wrote. His grammar and spelling have not been changed.

Irvin B. Hamilton letter to his wife

Dear Wife: I write you a few lines to let you know that I am well though I just came off duty. I stood guard 24 hours ____ no ____ and don't feel very well. We have got a plenty to eat. So far I have got nothing to write you yet. We have formed the militia that we have got here. They have got enough of them to form three regiments, three battalions and three companies ____ ____ give us to generate ____ for the emergency. I don't know how long we will have to stay in service. I am afraid we will have a hard road to travel before long, though I am easily scared when I think of the women. We are near enough to the Yankees to hear their guns. The wounded come in every day. G. W. Bowen is sick too. I think a little better.

I want you to hurry up Brown and send Ephraim Yawn on with the petition to the Governor and get all the signs [signatures?] on it you can. I think you can get me home if you work right and fast. When you write to me direct your letter to I. B. Hamilton in care of Capt. J. J. Lee, the First Georgia Militia Regiment, Atlanta, Ga. Nothing more this time only I am your [dear] husband to death. I. B. Hamilton

---

The "Brown" he referred to in the letter was most likely his brother Benjamin Brown Hamilton, who was a Colonel of Georgia Militia and in whose home near Cordele, Gov. Brown would stay after fleeing the Union troops later that year when they occupied the state capital in Milledgeville. Some of his descendants believe that his mother, Elizabeth Brown Hamilton, was related to Gov. Brown, but that has not been proved.

On August 6, 1864, Irvin died of typhoid dysentery at a military hospital in Macon. In his wife's application for a Civil War pension which she made on April 18, 1891, she described the circumstances behind his death: "He [Irvin B. Hamilton] was attacked with dysentery while in camp at Atlanta, Georgia, from whense he was carried to the hospital at Macon, Georgia, where I visited him—arriving at Macon late in the afternoon, and my husband, the said Irvin B. Hamilton, died that night, which was the sixth day of Aug. 1864. He contracted the said disease of which he died while in the Army."

It must have been a lonely and sad trip back to their home in Pulaski County accompanied, it is believed, only by one of her slaves (possibly a man named Joe Hamilton), who drove her there and back. Here she was, a widow at the age of twenty nine, with five small children between one and twelve years of age. The future must have looked bleak to her, and, for many years, it probably was, as she coped with the problems and scarcities of the Reconstruction era. But she had a large supportive family on both sides and a substantial estate to live on, assuming she had good help.

Sarah Caroline, as she was baptized, Caroline as she was known, and 'Ca'line' as she was called, was considered a strong and forceful woman. She never remarried, remaining on her plantation for the rest of her life. After Irvin's death, his brother, John J., was appointed administrator of the former's estate. In December 1877, for the fee of $5, John, as administrator, granted to Caroline the following properties: "four lots of land containing more or less 810 acres on which she lives as well as the land formally known as the Weeks Plantation and later as the Hutto Place containing about 800 acres, both located in the 14th District." Both properties were deeded to her on the condition that, at her death, the land would be passed on to her five children.

One story passed down through the generations by the Hamilton family descendants is that when the war ended and the slaves were freed, many were confused about their rights, what to do and where to go and so on. One of the slaves, Joe Hamilton, now free, was able to help clarify the situation by offering them assurances they were free to stay or to go but that they would be better off staying. Most of the former slaves remained working on the plantation and, as a result, Caroline granted land to Joe Hamilton. He took the last name of Hamilton and today, descendants of the "black Hamiltons" still own and dwell on that land. A graveyard on that property is still being used by their families for burials.

When Caroline died in 1908, both her obituary and memoriam appeared in the local newspapers. The obituary stated that she had died of paralysis [stroke] at the home of her son, Bartlett, in Chauncey, a small town south of Eastman. Three of her five children survived her. The obituary contained the following words:

"Mrs. Hamilton was a member of the Baptist Church and was a consecrated Christian, faithful to every duty of life and universally loved by all who knew her."

The memoriam which appeared one week later in the same Dodge County newspaper said this about her. "Ever anxious of the duties of life, answering its every call, she was at this post when the Reaper called for her soul to waft it to the eternal heavens. There was no idling for her, no wasteful sleep. She was up attending to her domestic affairs when stricken with that dreadful and almost always fatal malady, paralysis. She was one of the true women of olden times, as it were—the same dear face and tender voice each day, the same great character filled the smoothness and gifts that God alone can give. She fully realized the end was near, that in just a little while she would come to her reward, her crown, her home— finished the toil, the rest begun, the battle fought, and victory won."

Irvin is buried in the now destroyed Hamilton Family Cemetery on the outskirts of Eastman and Caroline is buried beside him, albeit 44 years later.

Children of Irvin Brown Hamilton and Caroline Lee

1. **Elizabeth, b. Feb 28, 1852; d. Apr. 18, 1933; m. Larkin Hargrove on Nov 23, 1871.**

2. William S., b. 1850; d. unk; m. Mary J. Brown on Oct 22, 1876.

3. Bartlett Benjamin, b. Sep 25, 1857; d. Sep 19, 1930; m. Leila Bradford on Sep 10, 1892.

4. John D., b. Sep 17, 1859; d. Jul 28, 1883; m. Fannie H. Edwards on Jan 31, 1883.

5. Pheraby, b. Mar 31, 1863; d. Jun 30, 1926; m. John James Harrell on Jun 24, 1877.

The Hendley Lineage

Information about the Hendley family is sparse. It is believed that an Elmore Hendley left Scotland with his wife, Sophia, and other family members, including a son named William, arriving in Virginia sometime before the Revolutionary War. Marilu Burch Smallwood, who researched this line extensively, claims: "It stands to reason that he was descended from the Hendley family of Lancaster County, England, as Lancaster County is only separated from Scotland by Cumberland County Eng., a distance of less than 60 miles, 'as the crow flies.'" She offers no real proof or any information on his direct lineage, so at best, this is a pure hypothesis. At this point we can say no more.

William Hendley

William was born about 1759 in Scotland and came with his family to Virginia before the Revolutionary War. He enlisted as a private in the Continental Army on February 14, 1777, and joined Capt. William Moseley's Company of the 7th Virginia Regiment of Foot on May 19, 1777. He signed up for the duration of the war. In August 1777 he was promoted to Corporal, then to Sergeant in February 1779, a rank he kept until being mustered out. Unit rolls show that he was on furlough from November 1777 to May 1778 during which time he reported in at Valley Forge. The 7th Regiment was renamed the 5th Regiment during the reorganization in September 1778. His unit moved the following month to Paramus, New Jersey, then to Camp White Springs, New York, then in succession to Newark, Princeton and Middlebrook, New Jersey, where it probably spent the winter at the last place. During the summer of 1779 his unit was stationed at Smith's Clove, where, like other units in the northern theatre of operations, it was inactive owing to a lack of military confrontations that summer.

In the fall of 1779 William's regiment was ordered to South Carolina to form part of the defense of Charleston. The Continental Army was defeated there, and the city fell to the British on May 12, 1780. William's regiment and his company's soldiers were made prisoners, and the enlisted men, like William it is assumed, were confined to British ships in the Charleston harbor. Later, all the Continental officers and men were paroled on the condition they would not rejoin the Continental Army. There are no military records for William after his parole so it is assumed that his fighting days were over.

After the war he moved with his father to Granville County, North Carolina, where he is found in the 1800 census. William married Amelia Ann (Milly) Horton, the daughter of David Horton and Ann (maiden name unknown) probably in Granville. For many years it was assumed that the David Horton named here was a descendant first of all from Barnabas Horton, an emigrant who settled in Long Island, New York. Then after that lineage was generally disproved, Thomas Horton, also an emigrant who settled in Springfield, Connecticut, was designated the ancestor of this line. Both had descendants, five generations down, named David

Horton, born about 1740/50. Up until days prior to putting this history to bed, I came across information that disproved not only that Thomas was not our ancestor but that there was a David Horton, the son of Joseph Horton, of Granville County, North Carolina, who left a will that proved, incontrovertibly in my opinion, he is our ancestor, and the father of Amelia Ann Horton who married William Hendley. Other information also showed that Joseph was the son of Daniel Horton, who emigrated from England in 1674 to Virginia as an indentured servant.

Nevertheless records show that this David Horton of Granville County served during the Revolutionary War. Records show conclusively that he supplied provisions to the Continental Army in Wake County. For that reason alone he is listed in the *DAR Book of Patriots*. One researcher, Adeline White, claims that in 1776 he served as a soldier in the 1st Southern Battalion of Militia under Colonel Ambrose Ramsey and marched against hostile Indians in Western Carolina. Smallwood points out that David Horton is listed in the *Roster of Soldiers from North Carolina*. Further she writes that he enlisted in August 1776 in the Orange County militia.

Shortly after the 1800 census was taken, William Hendley relocated from North Carolina to Bulloch County, Georgia. In December 1805 he was commissioned a captain of a militia unit of riflemen attached to the 51st Battalion, and in February 1806 he was once again commissioned a captain in another militia district in a part of Bulloch that would become Telfair County. About 1808 he relocated to Montgomery County in that part of the county that later became Telfair. He served on the first grand jury in Telfair which was for the April term of 1810, and later he was a justice of the peace for the 339th District. His home and farm were located in the Copeland area of Telfair on the road to the Old Daniel's Church.

After a few years resident in Telfair, William resettled in adjacent Pulaski County, where in 1818 he appeared as a tax payer. He put down roots on a piece of land about two miles north of Rhine, Georgia, where he built a home in which he lived until his death. He gave land for the Old Allston Methodist Church near his home. This church was later moved into Rhine and renamed the Rhine Methodist Church. William, his wife and children were members of the Hopewell Baptist Church which was located a couple of miles from Rhine on the Old Ocmulgee River Road in Pulaski, later Dodge County.

His will was dated November 22, 1836, and was probated on September 7, 1837, indicating that he probably expired sometime in 1837 when he was about seventy seven. His wife Milly was thought to have died around 1850, but that is not a sure thing. They are buried on their property in Dodge County.

Children of William Hendley and Amelia Ann (Milly) Horton

1. Sarah, b. 1792; d. unk; m. John Hayes on Nov 6 in 1809.
2. Nancy, b. Apr 22, 1793; d. unk; m. James Roundtree on Mar 16, 1823. They were among the first four families to settle in the newly formed Lowndes County, Georgia, in the early 1820s. James was robbed and murdered near Tallahassee, Florida, in 1837 while en route to the salt works on the Gulf of Mexico.

3. **Horton, b. 1795; d. Aug 22, 1872; m. Polly Ann Daniel on Aug 22, 1819.**

4. Mary, b. Jul 11, 1797; d. July 12, 1872; m. Joseph Fletcher on Jan 23, 1813.

5. Elizabeth, 1801; d. unk; m. Nehemiah Posey.

6. William, Jr., b. Dec 7, 1805; d. Jul 26, 1888; m. Sarah Harrell in 1833.

7. Millie, b. 1807, d. unk; m. unk.

8. Martha, b. 1808; d. unk; m. 1st Simon Bardin on Jan 10, 1828 and 2nd Alfred Belote in Sep 1837.

9. Jeanette, b. Feb 6, 1810; d. May 6, 1893; m. unk.

10. Sophia, b. Mar 9, 1813; d. Apr 24, 1879; m. William Holt Harrell on Oct 20, 1831.

Horton Hendley

Horton was presumably named for his grandfather, David Horton. He was born in North Carolina and moved to Georgia with his parents. In 1819 he married Mary Ann (Polly) Daniel, the daughter of Arthur Daniel and Sarah Waters, in Pulaski County. They lived near the Parkerson Baptist Church, as they were members of that church. During the War of 1812 he was a private in Capt. William Cooley's Company of Georgia Militia, serving at Fort Clark during August of 1813 and at Fort Adams in September of that same year. Between June 1825 and August 1827 Horton served as captain of militia in the 349th District of Pulaski County.

When he was seventy seven, he drowned in Gum Swamp Creek on his plantation and his body was never recovered. His wife,

Polly, was buried in an unmarked grave on the plantation of her grandson, James Daniel Harrell, in Dodge County.

Children of Horton Hendley and Mary Ann (Polly) Daniel

1. Sarah A. Dec 27, 1820; d. Jun 16, 1907; m. Uriah Keene on Dec 20, 1840.

2. Jeanette, b. Nov 8, 1822; d. Dec 6, 1882; m. John A. Harrell on Feb 19, 1846.

3. **Nancy, b. Jul 24, 1824; d. Oct 15, 1920; m. Andrew Jackson Hargrove on Sep 28, 1843.**

4. James Daniel, b. Jul 24, 1826; d. unk; Miss Jernigan (?)

5. Sophia, b. Mar 19, 1828; d. Jul 10, 1910; m. Willis Harrell on Apr 18, 1850.

6. Millie, b. Mar 1830; d. before 1856; m. William Taylor on Mar 4, 1852

7. William Horton, b. Jul 16, 1832; d. Jun 6, 1878; m. Mollie Caruthers on May 2, 1864.

8. John A., b. Aug 14, 1834; d. Dec 19, 1871; m. Edna Harrell on Jul 15, 1856.

9. Elizabeth, b. May 22, 1837; died young.

10. Mary, b. Mar 9, 1839; d. Dec, 1885; m. Matthew Clark on May 25, 1861.

The Lee Lineage

There were two Lees who came to the Virginia/Maryland area of Colonial America about the same time, the early 1640s. The more well-known of the two is Richard Lee, whose descendants include Richard Henry Lee and his brother, Francis, both signers of the Declaration of Independence; Gen. Light Horse Harry Lee and his son Gen. Robert E. Lee; and President Zachary Taylor. As one might expect this Lee line has been extensively researched and well-documented, and it can be safely said that we are not in that lineage. Period, no discussion. The other Lee is Hugh Lee. While his line is not as well-known, it is still fairly prominent and has a very interesting and historic background. Nevertheless, one researcher, Nan Overton West, who has written so clearly about her Lee family history, concludes with this statement, "No family in our lineage has passed so many traditions down to us while leaving researchers so perplexed and frustrated by the scarcity of documentation in existence." However she and others still believe that, while the documentation is often sketchy, the many different sources have provided enough circumstantial evidence that the Hugh Lee family has been established as our ancestor.

That family is the one founded by Hugh Lee, born about 1618. He emigrated from Shrewsbury, Shropshire, England, in about 1645 and settled in St. Mary's County, Maryland, and later Northumberland County, Virginia. He married a widow, Hannah Hewitt, maiden name unknown, and had at least one son, also named Hugh Lee. Their home in St. Mary's was once used for state assembly meetings and later sold to the state of Maryland; it still stands today. Their son, Hugh, Jr., was born in about 1650/51 in Northumberland County and died in about 1739 in Charles County, Maryland. He married Ann Barnett about 1673. Their son was William Lee, who was born on June 23, 1683, in Brunswick County, Virginia, and died there in 1761. He married Rebecca

Burchet and they had a son named William, Jr., born about 1715 in Brunswick County and died between 1764 and 1774 in Virginia. He married Elizabeth Ann Westbrook about 1735.

Up until this point there may be some debate about this Lee line being our ancestral line although it seems to be quite realistic and logical and, of course, is fairly well documented. With the birth in about 1740 of Samuel Lee, the son of William Lee, Jr., and his wife, Elizabeth Ann, in Brunswick County, the lineage from here on is very much clearer and neater. Samuel married, but the name of his wife is unknown. He relocated to Johnston County, North Carolina, where he died in early 1831. His son was William Lee, born about 1764 in Johnston County, who relocated to Chambers County, Alabama, where he died in August 1841. He married Zelpha, maiden name unknown. They were the parents of our Billy Lee, below.

William Lee

William "Billy" Lee was born in North Carolina in 1803, the son of William Lee, Sr. and his wife, Zelpha. Billy married Phereby Fail (also spelled Fale or Faile) in Johnston County, North Carolina, on November 27, 1827. Phereby was born about 1811 in North Carolina. She was the daughter of Jonathan Fail, who was born about 1782 and died, date unknown, in Pulaski County, Georgia, and his wife, Sally, maiden name unknown, who was born on July 22, 1780, and died about 1846 in Pulaski. Both were born in North Carolina.

Billy probably moved to Georgia in the mid-1830s along with his Fail in-laws. Census records show that his oldest son was born in North Carolina in 1832 while his second oldest child was born in Georgia in 1835. The *History of Dodge County* states that "During the year 1840 Billy Lee built the first house within the limits of what is now Eastman, about where the residence of the Judge James Bishop now stands." This is the area of Pulaski County that was cut out in 1870 to form Dodge County. Even today this part of the county is known as the Lee Voting District. Some of this land abuts the railroad line, and, in fact, on July 4, 1863, Billy transferred ownership of a strip of land in Lot 9, 15th District to the Macon and Brunswick Railroad.

The fact that he wrote his will on November 27, 1862, and recorded it on February 13, 1866, indicates that he probably died in early 1866. He named most of his living children as his heirs, and in the case of his married daughters, he included the names of their husbands, as well as those of several grandchildren whose parents had died by then. He did not mention his wife in the will which implies that she had preceded him in death. It is assumed that Billy and Phereby Lee are buried in unmarked graves on their property.

Children of William (Billy) Lee and Phereby Fail

1. Eli Franklin, b. Aug 6, 1832; d. Nov 1, 1892; m. Joanna Harrell on Oct 9, 1853.

2. **Sarah Caroline, b. Jun 25, 1835; d. Mar 18, 1908; m. Irvin Brown Hamilton on Oct 30, 1849.**

3. Levina, b. 1836; d. unk; m. Micajah Wright on Oct 29, 1849. Note that Levina was married one day before her sister, Sarah Caroline.

4. William L., b. 1837; no information.

5. Jonathan F., b. 1839; no information.

6. Emily Delanie, b. Feb 6, 1841; d. Mar 8, 1912; m. John A. Harrell on Jul 10, 1856.

7. Elizabeth, b. 1842; d. Sep 16, 1917; m. Charles N. Mullis on Feb 27, 1856.

8. Phereby, b. 1844, d. 1917; m. Alfred Mullis on Oct 8, 1857.

9. Talitha, b. 1845; no information.

10. Moses, b. 1848; no information.

11. Joanna, b. 1850; d. between 1758/59.

12. Sampson, b. 1851; d. Aug 5, 1911; m. Nancy Harrell on Mar 13, 1873.

Chapter 3

Wiregrass Country
The Shaw Family

Family Tree for
Lowndes Walton Shaw: Wiregrass Country
4 Generations

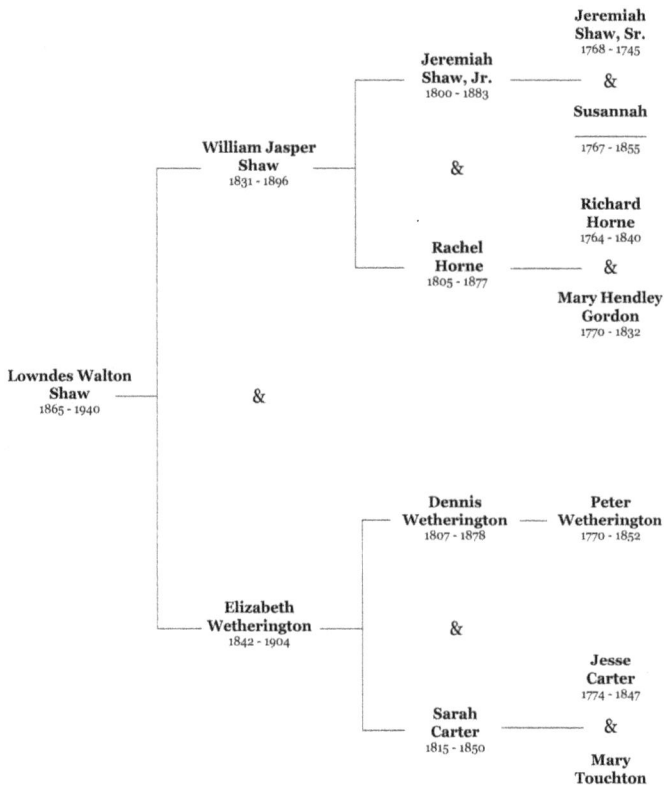

Lowndes Walton Shaw
1865 - 1940

&

William Jasper Shaw
1831 - 1896

Jeremiah Shaw, Jr.
1800 - 1883

&

Rachel Horne
1805 - 1877

Jeremiah Shaw, Sr.
1768 - 1745

&

Susannah
1767 - 1855

Richard Horne
1764 - 1840

&

Mary Hendley Gordon
1770 - 1832

Elizabeth Wetherington
1842 - 1904

Dennis Wetherington
1807 - 1878

&

Sarah Carter
1815 - 1850

Peter Wetherington
1770 - 1852

Jesse Carter
1774 - 1847

&

Mary Touchton

Chapter 3

Wiregrass Country
The Shaw Family

The tall grass that grows profusely under the dense pine tree forests of South Georgia is known as "wiregrass." Nowhere does it—or, perhaps it should be said, did it—grow so well as in that part of the state in and around Lowndes County. It is a hardy plant that thrives in the partial shade of the tall pines. It is very resistant to drought, fire, man and beast, especially the piney-woods pigs and raw-bone cattle that roamed the woods. At the end of the

Revolutionary War and as the inland areas of the Southeast section of the country began to open up, many settlers from North and South Carolina found that this area was perfect for raising their herds of cattle, goats and sheep, their principal source of wealth. All four of the families in this line—Shaws, Wetheringtons, Carters and Hornes—some with deeper roots in the area than others, lived here and thrived, although they did not always realize how tough it was, at least in our modern-day eyes.

The Shaw Lineage

A number of Shaw descendants and genealogists have tried to determine the family origin of Jeremiah Shaw, Sr., our earliest known Shaw ancestor, but their successes have been limited. The most plausible explanation has been put forth by Col. Milton Weeks, one of Jeremiah's descendants and a fine researcher. He took as a starting point that Jeremiah was in South Carolina before coming to Georgia by noting that census records showed that his first three children were all born between 1796 and 1800 in that state. He also noted that the names Bartley and Martin show up as a given name, once even together, with some frequency in the Shaw family line. In District 96, one of the seven districts then comprising South Carolina, there was a Captain Bartley Martin who had, according to census records, several daughters in the same age bracket as Jeremiah.

Coincidently there was a John Shaw living in the same section of District 96 who had a brother named Daniel although nothing more is known about those two brothers. But we do know that Jeremiah Shaw, Sr. named his first two sons John and Daniel, while another was named Bartley Martin. Therefore all the empirical evidence demonstrates that Jeremiah's parents were this John Shaw who married an unnamed daughter of Capt. Bartley Martin. Given that there are at least five other John Shaws in South Carolina during that time in history, it is futile even to try to figure out who John Shaw's parents were. This is not as conclusive as one would like but it is the best answer so far.

Jeremiah Shaw, Sr.

Jeremiah Shaw, Sr. was born on April 27, 1768, probably in that part of District 96 in South Carolina that later became Edgefield County. His father is not known; however, as noted above, some researchers have claimed it likely that he was the John Shaw who had married a daughter of Bartley Martin. While still living in that state, he married Susannah, maiden name unknown. Contrary to some family claims, there is no evidence that he served in the Revolutionary War, in so far as he was only thirteen years old when the war ended in South Carolina.

Based on the birthdays of his children he moved to Georgia between 1800 and 1803. The first mention of Jeremiah in any record was in 1813 minutes of Jones Creek Baptist Church in Liberty County, Georgia, which noted that he was member number 29. Jeremiah registered for the 1820 Land Lottery in that same county and drew Lot 38, Section 22, in Early County, Georgia, later Decatur County. That same year Jeremiah applied for and received a state land grant for 150 acres. While the precise location of this grant is unknown, it was situated in the western portion of Liberty County in what is now Long County.

Jeremiah appears to have been something of a disorderly member of the Jones Creek Baptist Church because of his apparent penchant for drinking. In late 1826 he was excommunicated from that church because of this failing. His public apology to the church on October 22, 1826, "that he had been drunk but was sorry for it," enabled him to remain a member in good standing. But on December 6th of that same year Jeremiah requested a "Letter of Dismissal" from the church and it was granted, perhaps because he had not been able to control his drinking. No subsequent membership in this church or any other church has been found.

That the church was strict with its "sinful" members and backed it up with punishment can be seen from an incident in 1824 between Jones Creek Church members Jeremiah Shaw and Richard Horne, whose son and daughter, respectively, had just married. The church minutes of September 25 report that, "Brother Jeremiah Shaw laid a complaint against Bro. Horn and accuses him of lying. Brother Light Townsend appointed to cite Bro. Horn at next conference." On November 27, "the case of Bro. Shaw and Bro. Horn: Bro. Horn arose and said it was a mistake in his speaking or in Bro. Shaw's hearing, but after much debate it appeared that Bro. Horn was in the wrong, and the question arose whether Bro. Horn should be expelled or not and being put to a vote, it was decided he should be expelled." Tough justice, but just two years later, as seen above, Jeremiah left the church just because of his drinking.

In early 1827 Jeremiah and most of his family moved to Decatur County, Georgia, and settled on the land he had acquired in the 1820 Land Lottery. Two of his sons, John and Jeremiah, Jr.

(Jerry), remained with their families in Liberty County while his remaining children and his son-in-law, George Harnage, who had married his daughter, Anna, made the move with him.

The tax rolls in Decatur County record that Jeremiah Shaw was exempt from the poll tax but was taxed on the 250 acres that he drew in the 1820 Land Lottery. During that time his sons, including Daniel K., Bartley, Levi and Elijah, paid poll taxes on various properties and other assets that they, obviously, had acquired somehow. County tax records indicate that Jeremiah was in the county from about 1827 to about 1834.

In about 1835 Jeremiah and his sons Daniel and Levi and his son-in-law, George Harnage, moved to Lowndes County, Georgia. As Jeremiah and his wife were then in their late 60s and did not own any property, it is likely that they lived with their son Daniel who owned property along the Little River in the 12th District. On August 1836 Jeremiah and his sons Jerry and Levi were among the signers of a petition addressed to the Governor of Georgia, protesting the pillage and destruction caused by Indians moving through the county.

The circumstances concerning his death are somewhat mysterious. There is no reason to believe that he did not live out his life in Lowndes County, yet he died in Liberty County in the home of his son John. The most likely explanation is that he was visiting John when he was taken ill and died at 4 PM on July 5, 1845, according to John's Bible.

His wife, Susannah, continued to live in Lowndes County, probably in the home of her son, Daniel. About 1846 Daniel moved to Hamilton County, Florida, and Susannah went with his family. In the 1850 census for Hamilton County she is listed as a member of Daniel's household, with her age given as eighty three and place of birth as South Carolina. Susannah became a member of the Prospect Baptist Church in that county. In 1854 she moved to Clinch County, Georgia, the home of her son Jerry. The following year, surrounded by her family, Susannah died of the infirmities of her age. John's family Bible records her death as "Susan Shaw, consort of Jeremiah, died in Clinch County, Georgia, the 9th of November 1855, age not fully known but supposed to be near 90 years." Both are buried in Long County, Georgia, not far from the Elim Baptist Church in a small family plot, identified as N31.80350 W081.69238 on a GPS. There are only six or seven graves there.

Children of Jeremiah Shaw, Sr. and Susannah (unknown last name)

1. John, b. Jun 6, 1796; d. Feb 2, 1863; m. 1st, Neoma _____ and 2nd Sarah Harnage in 1826.

2. Daniel K., b. 1797; d. 1863; m. Elizabeth _____ in 1823.

3. **Jeremiah, Jr. (Jerry) , b. Mar 20, 1800; d. Apr 8, 1883; m. Rachel Horne in 1824.**

4. Anna, b. Oct 5, 1803; d. Mar 12, 1877; m. George Harnage.

5. Bartley Martin, b. 1805; d. Aug 17, 1857; m. Matilda Horton on Jan 1, 1833.

6. Eleanor, b. 1807; d. 1860; m. Logan Sanders on Aug 21, 1828.

7. Elijah, b. May 9, 1810; d. Mar 11, 1854; m. Mary Thomas in 1843.

8. Levi, b. Sep 13, 1813; d. Dec 25, 1887; m. Susannah Hunter in 1840.

9. Mary, b. unk; d. Sep 16, 1848; m. Mr. Clark.

Jeremiah Shaw, Jr.

Jeremiah, or Jerry as he was always called, was born in South Carolina in 1800 and moved with his parents to Liberty County, Georgia, in the early 1800's. He married Rachel Horne in about 1824 in that same county. She was the daughter of Richard Horne, who had moved to Liberty County from Beaufort, South Carolina, after the Revolutionary War. Jerry and Rachel were still in Liberty County when the 1830 Census was taken, but shortly afterwards moved to Lowndes County, where their oldest son William Jasper was born in 1831. There Jerry acquired 490 acres of land in the 10th District, which is about three miles from Ray City, Georgia, and became part of Berrien County when it was cut out of Lowndes. But he was living in nearby Clinch County when his mother came to visit him in 1854, and it was in his home that she died the next year. Jeremiah was baptized in the Jones Creek Baptist Church in Liberty County. Later both he and Rachel were baptized in 1845 at the Union Primitive Baptist Church near Lakeland, where they were lifetime members.

Jerry was a farmer. It is not known how much land he owned although at one time or another he held ownership in three land lots, each one with 490 acres. He acquired land lot 499 as shown above, but in his will, he mentions land lot 500 in the 10th District which is adjacent to lot 499. Also, just two years before his death he sold one-half of land lot 235 in the 11th District, consisting of 245 acres, to his son-in-law, Jesse Moore, for $400, or $1.66/acre.

From 1823 to 1824 Jerry served as a 1st Lieutenant in the 16th Military District of Liberty County. During a two month period beginning on August 15, 1838, he served in Capt. Knight's militia company in order to help protect his community from Indian depredations.

Life in Lowndes County in the two decades or so after the area was settled seemed uncommonly harsh to an outside observer. Dr. J. R. Motte, a native of Charleston, South Carolina, educated at Harvard, and a surgeon who served in the U. S. Army during the 2nd Seminole War, was bivouacked several weeks in the fall of 1836 in Lowndes County. He wrote in his memoirs of his time in South Georgia, "Never have I met a more ignorant people who stood in more earnest need of school masters. They actually knew nothing beyond the necessity of eating to support life and of being clothed to defend themselves from the weather—mere vegetables. Their huts, with but few exceptions, you could hardly have induced a sensible dog to occupy, with his shedding tears of dissatisfaction and making strong opposition. And yet, so true it is, that 'ignorance is bliss', these people seemed contented, and knew not but that they possessed their amount of earth's luxuries." He goes on to say, "Put a rifle into the hands of the piney-wood settler, however, and as long as squirrels and deer are not extinct he is owner of the world in his estimation." In some ways, with respect to the latter observation, we have made little progress today.

After Rachel's death, Jerry married Sarah L. Howard, a widow, on December 5, 1879. Apparently this second marriage did not please him for he expressed the following so clearly in a codicil to his will, ". . .one certain widow Sarah L. Howard of Liberty County, Georgia, who has refused to fulfill her marriage vows to love, serve and obey me, neglecting to administer to my desire and wishes as a reasonable wife should do, therefore I give and bequeath to her, my present wife, the said Sarah L. Howard formerly but now Sarah L. Shaw, the sum of Five Dollars only, believing that she deserves nothing, having never assisted me in the accumulation of the property with which a kind providence has blessed, but it was made during the long and pleasant marital relations between me and my former beloved wife, whose name was Rachel Shaw, whose love and loving kindness I enjoyed for over fifty years. . ."

Yet there was one blot on Jerry's record. When Jerry was only seventeen years old he fathered a little girl. In a Recognizance (obligation) that both Jerry and his father signed on November 24, 1818, which was recorded in Liberty County Inferior Court records, he agreed to "maintain, support and educate a girl child born the 28th of January last, parta [born] of Sarah Morgan a single woman of this County and sworn to the said Jeremiah Shaw, Jun. as being the putative father. . ." The recognizance further stipulates that this obligation will remain in force until the girl reaches fourteen years of age. We do not know whether this obligation was kept, nor do we know what happened to the little girl or Sarah. We do know that the two of them must have been better off because of Jerry's latter action. He could have skipped town.

Rachel, the daughter and granddaughter of Revolutionary War soldiers and about whom we know little, comes off pretty well in the eyes of her husband. She must have been one of those extraordinary pioneering women of that era, raising fifteen of sixteen children to adulthood, and all the while keeping home and helping her husband operate their farm. All that just does not seem possible today.

Jerry and Rachel are buried In the Old Union Church Cemetery in Lanier County, Georgia, just in front of what used to be the Baptist church but, since 1998 has been used as a community center. This is the same church that was built on Jesse Carter's land way back in 1827. The cemetery is located south of Lakeland off Hwy 135 on Burnt Church Road.

Children of Jeremiah Shaw, Jr. and Rachel Horne

1. Rachel Letitia, b. Aug 14, 1825; d. Mar 10, 1883; m. Emanuel Studstill in 1846.

2. Irene S. (twin), b. 1826; d. 1889; m. Henry H. Hughes in 1842.

3. Mary (twin), b. 1826; d. Aug 8, 1884; m. Isaac McFadden.

4. Jeremiah J., b. Mar 24, 1829; d. Aug 8, 1862; m. Sarah Caroline Hughes. Records show that on July 1, 1862, he enlisted in the Confederate Army at Doctorstown in Liberty County, Georgia; however, he died at his home in Berrien County a little more than one month later. Did he contract a disease at the camp?

5. Richard James, b. 1830; d. Aug 9, 1869; m. Elizabeth Parker on Jan 18, 1849. One of Richard's great granddaughters is Emily Shaw Anderson, a close friend of the Valdosta Colemans. Her great-great-grandfather on her mother's side of the family is James Marion Pafford, the son of James Pafford and the brother of Tillithie Pafford Daughtrey, an ancestor of the Colemans (see Chapter 4 on the Paffords). This means that Emily and the

Colemans are double cousins, something that happens in small compact communities, generally more often in those days than now. Richard joined the Confederate Army in Doctorstown, Georgia, on May 7, 1862, and is last noted on the rolls of Company "F", 25th Regiment, in the 4th Quarter of 1863 when he drew a clothing ration. As noted he survived the war but died only four years after it ended.

6. **William Jasper, b. Apr 13, 1831; d. Aug 5, 1896; m. 1st Elizabeth Webb and 2nd Elizabeth Wetherington.**

7. Serena Ann, b. about 1833, d. unk; m. Elijah LaFayette Truitt.

8. Eleanor, b. Apr 6, 1835; d. Mar 23, 1854; m. Seaborn J. Sutton.

9. Nancy A., b. 1836; d. 1915; m. Benjamin Sirmans.

10. Lucy, b. 1838; d. unk; never married.

11. Matilda, b. Mar 2, 1840; d. Aug 29, 1913; m. Jesse Moore in 1865.

12. Malissie, b. 1842; d. unk; m. James J. Giddens on Sep 21, 1865.

13. John H., b. 1843; d. Apr 18, 1860; never married.

14. Elijah, b. 1844; d. 1862; m. Charlotte Smith on May 3, 1862. He enlisted in the Confederate Army on May 16, 1862, in Doctortown, Georgia. He was last noted on the rolls in October 1862 as being sick. He appears to have died while serving.

15. Francis Marion, b. Jan 5, 1846; d. Jan 1, 1922; m. Rachel Moore Allen in 1866. He enlisted in a regiment of Florida militia during the Civil War, where he fought at the Battle of Cedar Key, Florida, in July 1864. He was eighteen then and lost an arm at this battle yet survived to live to age seventy six.

16. Sarah Minerva, b. 1847; d. 1924; m. 1st James Frazier and 2nd Randall Folsom.

William Jasper Shaw

William was born in 1831 in the part of Lowndes County that became Berrien County in 1857. He farmed his entire life in the lower section of Berrien, not far from his father's land. His first wife was Elizabeth Webb, the daughter of Dawson and Frances Webb, who lived on a neighboring farm. Elizabeth probably died during or shortly after the birth of their only child, Malissa. William then married Elizabeth Wetherington about 1858, and they reared Malissa as well as ten children of their own.

William's life as a farmer, husband and father of three was interrupted by the onset of the Civil War. On April 27, 1862, he went to South Newport in Liberty County where he enlisted in the 1st Battalion of Georgia Cavalry ("Liberty Guards"). In January of 1863 the 1st Battalion consolidated with the 2nd Battalion to form the 5th Regiment of Georgia Cavalry which was a part of General Joseph Wheeler's Cavalry Division in the Army of the Tennessee. William's regiment saw service in all the Tennessee and Georgia campaigns during the last two years of the war, including all the battles preceding and including the Battle of Atlanta.

Records relating to William's military service are sparse. He is shown as "present" on Company "D" rolls for November and December 1863. The last existing record of him covers the period of June 30 to December 31, 1864, which states that he was "absent—detached as teamster in General Hood's Army." In 1864 Wm. J. Shaw was shown as a soldier in a militia unit in the 661st

Militia District, which encompassed Lowndes County. It is likely that he had left the Confederate Army in North Georgia after the fall of Atlanta and returned to his home. Was it because he was wounded or sick, or because his unit was essentially wiped out as a fighting force, or because he had gone AWOL? Regardless he continued to serve in a military unit but would never fight again since the war never came close to his home.

Only one story remains in the family concerning his Civil War service. William told his son, Lowndes, who in turn told one of his daughters, Virginia, that, on returning to his home, he found that it had burned, with his wife and three children living in a dirt floor shack. Finding his family in such a condition may be one reason he remained in South Georgia with a militia unit rather than returning to his original unit. No explanation was given as to why Elizabeth and the children were not taken into a relative's home.

After the war he returned to his farm and fields to support his growing family. Tax records showed that he owned 590 acres of land at Ray's Mill, near Ray City, on which he grew enough cotton to support his family. However, the hard times during reconstruction and the demands of his large family probably did not permit him to rise much above a subsistence level. The 1870 Census records the value of William's real estate at $300 while that of his other assets at $867, all of which indicate that he was far from being a wealthy man. The 1887 tax records show the value of his 590 acres at $1,302.

William was a member of the Cat Creek Primitive Baptist Church, joining on October 19, 1871, only four years after this church was founded. Located on Cat Creek Road in Lowndes County just three miles north of Bemis, it still has an active membership today. On March 4, 1876, he was ordained a deacon of this church, an office he held until his death.

He died while working the fields on his farm. The *Valdosta Daily Times* reported he "had been in good health up to two weeks ago, though he had reached the advanced age of nearly 65 years. He went to his field a week or so ago and pulled a row of fodder, after which he returned to his house in a very nervous condition, and has been confined to his bed since then, though hopes were entertained for his recovery up to Tuesday night. He had no fever and his illness was thought to have been a result of the excessive heat in the field where he had begun to work. His death removes one of the most prominent farmers in that section and a man who had won the confidence and esteem of all of those whom he came in contact."

Some two months after his death, the *Times* printed an obituary written by T. W. Stallings, a Baptist minister in Nashville, who wrote movingly about William's faith and his acceptance of God. In discussing the man and his character Stallings noted that William was "strictly an honest man. He was a good and noble citizen, as the community in which he lived can gladly testify, for his neighbors held him in the highest esteem. He was blest of the Lord to raise a good and most honorable family; which, together with his friends and neighbors can realize better today what he was worth, than before his death. . .The Church suffers too, for she had lost a great, good and useful member, as well as an officer. We beg that that the Lord in His mercy may bless and take care of his bereaved wife and children."

Soon after his death Elizabeth and her two unmarried daughters moved to Valdosta to live with her son Lowndes. She died there in 1904 at the age of sixty one. Her obituary in the *Valdosta Daily Times* stated that, "She was taken with the grip several weeks ago and that attack was followed by a complication of troubles. When the end came she was surrounded by all but two of her children. Her death had been expected for several days and during the time her family and friends had been very devoted in administering unto her....Mrs. Shaw was a woman of great will power and though she had been in ill health for fifteen years or more, she led an active life." Both William and Elizabeth are buried in the cemetery adjacent to the Cat Creek Baptist Church where they had worshiped for most of their adult lives.

Children of William Jasper Shaw, including the first born, Malissa, by Elizabeth Webb and the remaining by Elizabeth Wetherington

1. Malissa, b. Nov 10, 1857; d. Jun 9, 1934; m. George M. Devane on Aug 2, 1874.

2. Leonard F., b. May 25, 1859; d. Mar 1900; m. Sallie Giddens on Apr 11, 1884. Leonard became a businessman in Valdosta, served one term as a Valdosta city councilman and, along with his brother, Lowndes, donated the land for Drexel Park.

3. Ida Isabelle, b. 1861; d. Jan 4, 1927. m. Richard S. Johnson on Aug. 16, 1878.

4. **Lowndes Walton, b. Oct 2, 1865; d. Apr 30, 1940; m. Meta Aubrey Charles on Dec 16, 1909.**

5. Celestia Indiana, b.Oct 6, 1867; d. Oct 25, 1945; m. Dr. Jesse A. Parrish on May 21, 1890.

6. Lillie G., b 1869; d. 1930; m. William F. Mathis on Feb 25, 1892.

7. Texas Anna, b. Aug 7, 1871; d. Aug 1, 1919; m. Edwin Gaskins on Nov 26, 1890.

8. William B., b. Apr 11, 1873; d. Mar 27, 1915; m. Frances Bullard on Jan 10, 1892.

9. Georgia A., b. Sep 29, 1875; d. Mar 6, 1920; m. William A. Moore on Jun 15, 1893.

10. Beulah, b. Nov 15, 1877, d. May 18, 1936; m. W. A. Sims.

11. Ora Lee, b. Sep 14, 1881; d. Aug 3, 1965; m. Roy Knight, Oct 14, 1902.

Lowndes Walton Shaw

Lowndes Shaw was truly a self-made man. He was born into a large Berrien County farming family of modest means only a few months after the Civil War ended. Early on he was put to work in the cotton fields like most other boys in the area. His formal education was roughly equivalent to a third-grade level. Yet Lowndes was clearly ambitious and wanted something more than he could achieve by just being a farmer. Since his father did not have the financial resources to help him, he planted cotton along the fence rows on the family farm to earn enough money to start out on his own. By the age of eighteen Lowndes had moved to Valdosta where he first lived with his older brother, Leonard and his wife, and where he began his new business career in partnership with him. The details of how he achieved his business successes are not known, but it is evident that he had a flair for business.

After his father died in 1896 Lowndes moved his mother and two youngest sisters into his home on East Central Avenue in Valdosta. He sent his two youngest sisters to college although neither graduated. His mother lived with him until her death and his sisters did the same until their marriage. Although his brother Leonard died relatively young at the age of forty two, he was able to continue to achieve economic success on his own, thereby improving his financial condition as well as his status in his adopted community.

Lowndes married relatively late in life when was forty four years old. His daughters always said he wanted to ensure that all his sisters were married and settled down before he followed suit. On Dec 16, 1909, he walked down the aisle with Meta Aubrey Charles, a charming young lady who was descended from a pioneer north Florida family and who was half his age. The *Valdosta Daily Times,* "the *Times,*" reported that they "were married in Jacksonville, Florida, at the home of the bride and that his family learned of his marriage from a telegram sent from Jacksonville to one of this sisters."

The article goes on to say, "The news will be quite a surprise to Mr. Shaw's many friends in Valdosta as his plans had not been revealed to any except one or two of his immediate relatives. He left here last Tuesday for Jacksonville, stating to two of his relatives at the time that he would come back a married man, but further than that he said nothing to anyone else. . .The bride is known to some of the people here, having lived in Lake City before moving to Jacksonville. She is very prominent in social circles, is accomplished and beautiful, and has a large circle of friends in the cities where she has lived."

Meta's father had died when she was not quite three-years old, leaving his wife, Meta's mother, in difficult financial circumstances. Therefore the family was split up, with Meta being sent to Jacksonville to live with her great aunt, Virginia Crews Harte, the sister of her grandmother, Mary Crews Charles. Until her marriage she would live largely in Jacksonville with Virginia although she would visit frequently with her mother, brother and sister in Lake City, a town about sixty miles away. It may have been in Virginia's home on Monroe Street that she was married.

The newly-wed couple moved into Lowndes's home in Valdosta where their first child was born. Shortly thereafter they moved into a smaller house that Lowndes had built on Magnolia Street almost directly behind his previous home. After a few years the family relocated to another house that he constructed on the east side of Ashley Street near the intersection with Jane Street which, at that time, was in the countryside and where they lived until 1919. This house was located on a large plot of land and had a barn for his horses and buggy, which later on was used as a garage for his Model T Ford. He also built a cottage behind his house, but distant from it, where a black couple and their young daughter lived. There was a large garden, a place to keep a few cows and, for a while, some hogs, as well as a big chicken yard. The black man tended the garden and animals.

Lowndes and Meta had three children. A boy was born first, but he died shortly after birth. His obituary in the *Times* stated movingly that, "The little son of Mr. and Mrs. Lowndes W. Shaw was called as a messenger of innocence to the better land this morning at an early hour, the little one's death occurring just a few hours after it was born. The child was apparently very healthy and the attending physician did not know what caused its death except that its circulation was bad. The remains will be interred this afternoon at four o'clock in the city cemetery." The baby was never named and his gravestone in their family plot simply states "Infant Son of L. W. and Meta C. Shaw". In 1911, a daughter, Virginia, named for her mother's great aunt, was born, and then in 1914, another daughter, Meta, named for her mother, came along.

Lowndes's first business, or at least an early business, was a hardware store on downtown Ashley Street which he owned and operated with Leonard, and later was managed by one of his brothers-in-law, W. A. Sims. In the 1896 Valdosta phone book, Shaw Brothers, Merchants, had the number "6" which was the same number as the hardware store. That same year he and Leonard became charter investors in the A. S. Pendleton Company, a wholesale grocery business. The Model Bakery, the first of its kind in Valdosta, was another enterprise which he owned and operated with other investors between 1914 and 1937, and was managed by another brother-in-law, Roy Knight. He was one of the early organizers and shareholders of the Valdosta Street Railway Company, a business in which he took an active interest during the time it operated in the city. Lowndes also had an interest in Mathis and Shaw Furniture, a retail store.

He always wanted to work for himself, not for others, to be the boss and not be bossed. When Lowndes was an old man he admonished his nephew W. K. Weaver that he should never work for anyone else. His rationale was that the employer would always keep 90 percent of what you earned for him, your employer, and let you, the employee, keep only 10 percent. By all accounts Lowndes followed his own advice. As an entrepreneur he did not have a fixed office but, instead, he worked out of his home or from the premises of one of his businesses. He was frugal, never wasting a penny. He always carried with him a small notebook in which he wrote down every expenditure including any money given to one of his family members. Neither his wife nor his daughters received an allowance; when they needed money for something, they had to ask for it and, presumably, justify the need.

One day in 1911 Lowndes prepared a financial statement which somehow has been passed down through the years. It shows that his largest single asset was a 1,315 acre farm near Cherry Creek where Stalling Road meets Knight's Academy Road in Lowndes County. In addition he owned eleven parcels of land ranging from his part ownership of twenty five acres held by the Ashley Land Company to fourteen lots in Barrett, just north of Moody Air Force Base. He also held "Notes of all kinds," merchandise in several general stores, corporation stocks, livestock and other such assets. All together he valued those assets at $110,130. No debts were listed.

At the end of World War I, Lowndes, then fifty four, decided to try his luck in the real estate business in Miami where he became a land developer and speculator. A headline in the *Times* issue of October 31, 1919, reads, "Mr. Lowndes Shaw's Family Left Today for Miami". The first paragraph begins, "When Councilman Lowndes W. Shaw and his family left Valdosta this morning for Miami, making the trip in their automobile, the city lost a citizen who has measured up well in the duties of good citizenship." It goes on to point out some of his achievements mentioning that he had been a "live wire in business as well as city development." It further stated that "he is a city councilman and mayor pro-tem of the city at the present."

The first thing he did on arriving in Miami was to find a home and enroll his daughters in Northside Elementary School: Virginia in the first grade and Meta in kindergarten. Then he began to apply his business skills. His mode of operation was to find a builder who had run out of funds to complete the construction of a particular house. Lowndes would buy that house at a substantial discount, complete and furnish it, move his family into it and then put it up for sale. When that house was sold he would move his family out and start the whole process over. At times he would be working on several houses in different stages of completion.

His daughter Virginia remembers living in nine different houses during the seven years they lived in Miami. When he did not have a house in move-in conditions for the family, then they would live in an annex of the Peabody Inn, a Miami landmark, of which he was part owner. Each summer the family would make the long drive back to Valdosta where Lowndes would tend to his businesses and farm. One summer, however, they moved into a boarding house in North Georgia and another summer the family went to Hendersonville, North Carolina. After the summer break they would once again return to Miami to continue their life and his work there.

After leaving Miami in 1926 for that summer's break, Lowndes dropped off his family in White Springs, Florida, where Meta and their daughters moved into the Colonial Hotel. Lowndes then went on to Valdosta, where he supervised the construction of a large and impressive two-story house on a newly purchased 15 acre tract at 1115 N. Ashley Street, adjacent to his previous home on that same street. This was a "tabby" house, so called because broken coquina shells were embedded in the outside stucco walls. Lowndes travelled back and forth that summer to St. Augustine to pick up and deliver the shells, stopping on the way in White Springs to visit his family. When the house was finished, he gathered them up, and they moved into their new home in Valdosta. When they arrived that first evening they saw that he had completely furnished the house and that the newly hired cook had already prepared a hot dinner for them. It seemed the family was home to stay.

In September of 1926 a devastating hurricane, later referred to as the Great Miami Hurricane, made landfall, forcing Lowndes to return to Miami to check on his properties. As he approached the city the train on which he was travelling was sidetracked in Lemon City to let a Red Cross train through, leaving him unable to continue on. He got off the train and walked the remaining distance to one house he still owned on 27th Terrace NE and where he had left their effects from the previous year. The house had been completely flooded but, by arriving there in a timely manner, he was able to save most of the furniture and carpeting, including the piano which he dried thoroughly, thus keeping the veneer from buckling. This house was then sold and the furniture sent to Valdosta. This ended his Miami venture.

His older grandsons (he would have eight but lived to see only one) still remember with fondness the big house on Ashley Street. There was a magnificent Magnolia tree in the front yard that must have been put there just for boys to climb. The large backyard extended seemingly forever and was covered with fruit trees and bushes, including scuppernong grapes, pears, blueberries and huckleberries, with plenty of places to play and hide. It was also in this backyard that one of his grandsons gashed his knee on a hoe, blade facing up, that his thoughtless brother had left out. There was a smoke house and, earlier, a commissary where Lowndes sold goods to his farmers at cost. After Lowndes died, his wife divided the house, and the second story was converted to a rental apartment. Long-time tenants were Howard and Catherine Holt, the owners of the Pepsi Cola plant. During WWII their daughter Meta and her two sons moved in with her for about a year while Meta's husband was serving in the U. S. Army.

According to Lowndes's children, times were tougher during the worldwide Depression particularly given that he had not yet recovered from his losses due to the Florida hurricane. His income fell significantly and the value of his assets, like those of nearly everyone else, declined as well. He tightened his belt and survived the Depression but he never regained his previous level of wealth. Yet, there was still enough money to send both daughters away to fine universities, to buy Virginia a new car as her graduation present and to send Meta on a European tour as hers. And there was enough left upon his death to support his widow for the last twenty six years of her life.

From his earliest days in Valdosta Lowndes always met his civic responsibilities. At the age of eighteen he joined the Patterson Fire Company, a voluntary organization. A glance at the names of some other members of this company reveal that they were or would become some of the movers and shakers of his community—Pendletons, Varnadoes, Peeples, Converses and so on. In joining the company of such men early in life, he was laying the groundwork for a successful business career as well as serving his community.

In 1887 he became a member of the newly formed Company "B", 4th Infantry, Georgia State Troopers, also known as the Valdosta Vedettes. This voluntary militia company was a type of early National Guard but it also had a social aspect with public drills (very entertaining), picnics and fairs being an integral part of their activities. There is a photograph of Lowndes, then only twenty two, in his uniform, rifle at his side, chin held high and very serious. It is a picture of a young man who is going to amount to something.

At the turn of the twentieth century Lowndes was named a member of the committee that secured the Georgia State Fair for Valdosta. The front page of the *Times* highlighted the 1900 Fair and his photograph, along with the other committee members, forms the centerpiece of that page. An original copy of this newspaper edition is now in the possession of Richard Coleman, his grandson.

In one of his most commendable deeds, Lowndes, his brother Leonard's estate, and three other landowners donated in 1916 an eight plus acre tract of land at the intersection of Patterson Street and Brookwood Drive that they owned jointly to be used as a city park, with a part of this tract to be set aside for the construction of the Woman's Building to house the DAR, UDC and the Wymodausis Club. That park is now Drexel Park, and the deed to the city stipulates that it will revert to the donors or their heirs if the land were ever used for purposes other than that of a park. Drexel is still the largest park in the city and is expected to remain so as an oasis of peace and quiet—well, there is a children's playground now. An historical marker at the park recognizes their contribution.

Lowndes was elected for one term as a Valdosta City Councilman serving from 1918 to 1920. When he was in his late sixties he was sworn in as a member of the Lowndes County Commission, serving from 1933 to 1935. Like everything else in his life, he took his civic and community responsibilities very seriously. When he ran for re-election for this post, he was defeated—which was just as well since he might already have contracted the cancer that would kill him five years later.

Social activities were also important to him. Lowndes was a charter member of the first Elks Club established in Valdosta. Moreover, he was an active member of the Valdosta Chapter of the Royal Arch Masons #107, where he served in 1907 as Treasurer, Senior Warden in 1908 and Junior Warden in 1909, and, lastly, Worshipful Master in 1911 and 1912. After his marriage he appeared to tone down his social activities, probably to focus more on his family.

Lowndes was not a churchgoer. His parents and other family members were all "hard shell" Baptists and to join that church, one had to have a blinding revelation, which never happened to him. Just before his death he was baptized into the First Methodist Church, his wife's church. Regardless, he and his family would often attend the Big Meetings (revivals) held during the summers at the Cat Creek Baptist Church, his father's church, where several of his siblings were members.

His daughter Virginia wrote about those summertime Big Meetings she attended as a child: "All the farmers would be there with watermelons in their wagons. The preaching went on all morning and people would come and go, eat watermelons and socialize. We would then go to Aunt Isabelle's [Isabelle Shaw Johnson] for dinner. All the invited people would be served at a full table and then the table would be cleared and the next group would be served, and so on. The children were last and it was often around 5 o'clock before they would feed us. By that time I was so nauseated by a lack of food that I couldn't eat. Children were not first in those days."

Despite his relatively small stature Lowndes was a vigorous man. When he was almost seventy years old, he undertook a trip so unique that it was reported in the *Times*. One morning he drove from Valdosta to Athens, Georgia, where he had lunch with his daughter Meta, then turned around and drove back to Valdosta with Meta and two other Valdosta boys, Lamar Tillman and Omar Franklin, also attending the University of Georgia, arriving home at 7:10 P.M., a round trip that took about thirteen hours. According to the newspaper article he "found the roads somewhat slippery [many were unpaved] which cut down his driving speed somewhat." In another newspaper article he was paid a compliment when Meta was elected president of her university sorority. It said that, "Lowndes Shaw, country commissioner, has a daughter who is a chip off the old block. She has the same qualities of attracting friends to herself and inviting confidence in herself that Lowndes has."

By all accounts, Lowndes and Meta had a good married life. Even in tough times they had more than enough to be just comfortable. The large difference in their ages was something of a problem and Lowndes, twenty two years his wife's senior, sometimes treated her more like a daughter than a wife. He was in full control of his family. He never allowed his wife to learn to drive, assuming she wanted to do so, and he kept tight reins on the money that he had worked so hard to amass.

The children had a wonderful life. They took ballet and dance lessons as well as art and piano lessons. And they were always on the go. Their daughter Meta kept a diary when she was at Valdosta High School, and it reveals that they were constantly going over to friends' houses, meeting boys, playing bridge, going to dance parties, attending church, etc. Interestingly, her diary could easily have been written by a teenage girl today except, maybe, for the passage about going on a possum hunt. That their children were well reared cannot be in doubt.

After a long bout with cancer Lowndes died at the age of seventy four. His obituary was printed on the front page of the *Valdosta Daily Times*. The headline above his photograph read:

Lowndes Shaw Dies after Illness

Prominent Business and Civic Leader of
Valdosta Dies at Residence After Illness of
Some Time   Rites to be Tomorrow

As expected, Meta outlived Lowndes by many years. After WWII she rented their big house on Ashley Street and moved to a much smaller yet comfortable house on that same street just a block away. She spent the remainder of her life there. For a short time in the late forties, the big house was rented to Carson McLane, Inc. for its funeral operations, and one can see a photograph of it today at their premises on Patterson Street. After Meta's death her daughters sold the house and, some years later, it was razed and something rather hideous built in its place. Life goes on.

Meta led a quiet life oriented around her daughters, grandsons and many friends. She was an active member of the First Methodist Church. Her outside interests included memberships in the Garden Club and the Wymodausis Club. When canasta, a card game, became the rage in the 1950s she became an avid player and taught many of her grandchildren to play. She was also active in the UDC, her ancestor being Lt. Reuben H. Charles of the First Florida Cavalry. At one account of a UDC meeting it was reported in the local newspaper that "she was the envy of every women there. Her hair, as you know, is naturally curly. It was set in a pompadour fashion, off the forehead, and made a fitting halo for a sweet and charming face."

One of her great disappointments in life was not being able to identify a Revolutionary War ancestor so that she and her sister Ethel could join the DAR. During the 1920s and 1930s the two of them spent a considerable amount of effort in this search, even hiring professional genealogists to help. Alas, they were unsuccessful even though the information they collected has helped their descendants piece together their family history. They also prodded other family members to write them letters recounting events of the past including fascinating tales and incidents of family life in north Florida in the mid-1800s.

In 1964, while visiting her daughter in Ft. Myers, Florida, she died. She is buried beside her husband and infant son at Sunset Hill Cemetery in Valdosta.

Children of Lowndes Walton Shaw and Meta Aubrey Charles

1. Virginia Elizabeth, b. Dec 19, 1911; d. Jul 2, 2001; m. Alphonse Louis Girardin on Mar 28, 1934. Virginia received a bachelor's degree from Randolph-Macon Women's College in Lynchburg, Virginia and later a Master's in Medical Social Work from Case Western Reserve in Cleveland. She married Louie Girardin of Valdosta. After he completed his internship in pediatrics, they relocated to Ft. Myers, Florida, where he became the first pediatrician to practice along the southwest coast of Florida below Tampa. He served as a physician in the U.S. Army during WWII. Virginia assisted her husband in his medical practice, and after his untimely death in 1961, she was employed as a case worker for the State Adoption Agency until she retired. Virginia and Louis reared three sons: Jerry, Peter and David.

2. **Meta Aubrey Shaw, b. Apr 28, 1914; d. Oct 20, 1997; m. Theo Wade Coleman on Nov 12, 1938.**

The Wetherington Lineage

The first known Wetherington in this line, William, is believed to have lived in North Carolina but it is not known in which county he settled. At some point he moved his family to Cheraw District, South Carolina, to that part that later became Darlington County and where William is shown a member of the Buckhead Baptist Church. He was also granted one hundred acres of land there on Beaver Dam Creek in October 1784. Later in 1786 he paid three pounds ten shillings for 100 acres on Black Creek. Both of these properties were located in the Cheraws. He was still in that district in 1790 when he appeared in the census that year as the head of family. At some point afterwards he moved his family to Colleton County, South Carolina. This is about all that is known about William during his sojourn in South Carolina, and even that information might not be completely accurate. A William Witherington is also found in Dobbs County, North Carolina, who served in the Revolutionary War, but it is very doubtful that he is our William since he moved to Alabama. For future researchers: don't get them mixed up.

It is pretty much agreed that William was the father of Peter Wetherington and that both of them migrated to Georgia, albeit at different times. The first record of William was in December 1806 in Tattnall County, Georgia, where he was a party in a legal suit. The next year he served on a county grand jury. In 1809 he was asked to appraise the value of three cows. On December 8, 1810, he sent a letter to Jas. Berry, stating that "Sir, this comes to inform you that I have sent the money that them stray cows sold for by Robert Henry. Willm Wetherington." The last mention of him in the county records or anywhere else was his service in the May term of 1812 as a Tattnall County grand juror. We do not know his date of death, but he must have been an old man by 1812, so he probably died shortly thereafter since no further records on him are found. We do not know the name of his wife or any of his children except for Peter below.

Peter Wetherington

Peter, the son of William Wetherington, was born in South Carolina, the exact place is not known. He moved with his family to Darlington County, South Carolina, between 1785 and 1790 and later to Colleton District, South Carolina, where Peter married his first wife, name unknown. The first appearance of Peter in Georgia is when he shows up in Lowndes County in the winter of 1827-28 where he settled on a tract of land in the Grand Bay section of the county near Naylor.

It is believed that his first wife, with whom he had five children, died before he moved from Colleton County, South Carolina, to Georgia. He then married Esther, maiden name unknown, with whom he had four more children. Nothing more is found about him in county records simply because nearly all the Lowndes County records were destroyed when the courthouse burned in 1870.

Children of Peter Wetherington and first wife (five children), and second wife, Esther, (four children)

1. Curtis, b. 1800; d. unk; m. unk.
2. **Dennis, b. Oct 1, 1807; d. May 28, 1878; m. 1st Sarah Carter; 2nd Rebecca Roberts; and 3rd Elizabeth Roberts.**
3. Elender, b. Apr 3, 1813; d. May 19, 1889; m. John Lee
4. William, b. 1818; d. 1900; m. Margaret Sherley in 1836.
5. Benjamin, b. 1822; d. unk; m. Eleanor_____.
6. Peter, b. 1826; d. unk; m. Martha_____.
7. Rebecca, b. 1829; d. unk; never married.

8. Joseph, b. 1831; d. Apr 1, 1907; m. Eliza Wilkerson in July 1855.

9. John, b. Sep 20, 1833; d. Jan 1, 1896; m. Jane Wilkerson.

Dennis Wetherington

Dennis was born in South Carolina, probably in Colleton County, and moved with his parents to Lowndes County between 1825 and 1830. The 1830 Census shows him as the head of a two-person household consisting of one male, certainly Dennis, and one female, almost certainly, his wife, Sarah Carter, to whom he was recently married, their first child, Rachel, having been born later in October of 1831. Dennis had three wives. In addition to Sarah, with whom he had ten children, and who died in about 1850, he had two children with Rebecca Roberts. After her death, he had four children with wife number three, Elizabeth Roberts, who was also the sister of Rebecca Roberts, by then deceased. In all Dennis fathered sixteen children.

After marrying Sarah they moved to a farm near what is today Naylor, where Dennis, with his succession of wives, lived for the rest of his life. He was baptized into the membership of the nearby Union Church on February 11, 1832, and was dismissed in 1841 from that church by letter so that he could join in constituting the newly formed Unity Church which was closer to his home and to which he formally adhered on February 6, 1841.

Dennis was active in Lowndes County's community and civic affairs. In August 1836 he was one of seventy five local residents who signed a petition to the Governor requesting relief from the Creek Indians who were menacing them. Then he served as a private under Captain S. E. Swilley in the 2nd Regiment of Florida Militia for six months beginning June 16, 1837. This was during the Second Seminole War. He was a member of a commission appointed by the state legislature to identify and purchase a site for a new town on the newly constructed railroad line through Lowndes County which purchase took place at the end of 1859. He and the other three county commissioners plotted the site and then incorporated Valdosta on December 7, 1860.

During the Civil War, Dennis's name appears on the roster of the 661st Militia District. It noted that he was fifty six years old and a farmer. His son Matthew, seventeen, is also on this roster. This is the last mention of Matthew in any record, so he may be the M. Wetherington who served in Company "D" of the 50th Georgia Regiment of Infantry during the war and who is listed as "died." This unit was almost completely comprised of Lowndes County soldiers and was the same unit in which Matthew's brother Jesse served and, later, was killed at the Battle of Cedar Creek, Virginia.

Dennis and his third wife, Elizabeth along with other family members, are buried in the Wetherington family cemetery near Naylor on Grand Bay Road. The cemetery is somewhat difficult to find today although every now and then burials still take place. The GPS coordinates are N30.85208 W083.09932.

The following page contains the list of children belonging to Dennis Wetherington and his three wives. He fathered children by each of his wives. These children are designated with a collection of asterisks to denote their respective mothers.

Dennis Wetherington's daughter, Elizabeth, is our direct Wetherington ancestor. She married William Jasper Shaw in 1858.

Children of Dennis Wetherington by three wives. With first wife, Sarah Carter, there were ten children. With his second wife, Rebecca Roberts, two children are identified with one asterisk. Those with his third wife Elizabeth Roberts display two asterisks.

1. Rachel, b. Oct 5, 1831; d. unk; m. Mr. Farr.

2. Nancy, b. Apr 20, 1833; d. Feb 23, 1897; m. Richard A. Howell in 1851.

3. Mary, b. Dec 5, 1834; d. unk; m. John Fletcher.

4. Jesse, b. Sep 23, 1836; d. Mar 4, 1864; never married. He was killed at the Battle of Cedar Creek in Virginia.

5. Serena, b. Nov 27, 1838; d. Sep 11, 1911; m. Charles Rentz.

6. Molsy, b. Oct 1, 1840; d. unk; Washington Allred.

7. **Elizabeth, b. Aug 22, 1842; d. Apr 22, 1904; m. William Jasper Shaw in 1858.**

8. Sarah, b. Aug 3, 1843; d. unk; m. Isbin Green

9. Matthew, b. Dec 19, 1844; d. unk; m. unk.

10. Job Elbert, b. Feb 11, 1849; d. Apr 13, 1917; m. Sarah Ann Zeigler.

11. *Isham A., b. Oct 30, 1852; d. Sep 25, 1923; m. Marian M. Zeigler on Dec 3, 1874.

12. *Hansell, b. Apr 13, 1855; d. unk; m. Margaret Blanton

13. **Dawson Webb, b. Feb 18, 1857; d. unk; m. _____ Wetherington.

14. **George Powhatan, b. Nov 30, 1858; d. 1926; m. Remma Blanton

15. **Dennis Bartow, b. May 10, 1861; d. Nov 9, 1919; m. Rachel Zeigler.

16. **Perry Andrew, b. May 28, 1867; d. unk; m. Leila Touchton.

The Carter Lineage

The name Carter is one of the most common surnames both in England and in the U.S. but is particularly found in the South. All this makes it very difficult to trace one's ancestry in such a large family line. Nevertheless, Jacob Carter of South Carolina has been definitely documented as our first known Carter ancestor. Born about 1720, probably in Virginia, he moved through North Carolina, stopping for a while in Bertie County, before settling in Colleton County, St. Bartholomew's Parish, South Carolina, as is shown in the 1790 Census. He probably died in South Carolina sometime between 1790 and the end of the century.

We do not know the name of Jacob's wife or who definitely were his parents, but there are two candidates as his ancestor, both with the first name of Thomas. One is a Capt. Thomas Carter who immigrated to Virginia in 1652 and was a very prominent citizen in Lancaster County. It would be nice to have him as our ancestor since this line is related by marriage to George Washington, but that does not seem to be the case, even though a well-respected genealogist, Mary Ketus Deen Holland, who thoroughly researched Jacob Carter's descendants, makes this claim, albeit without giving much evidence. It is more likely that Jacob's ancestor was another Thomas Carter from Isle of Wight County, Virginia, although Mrs. Holland dismissed that possibility. Four sons of this large Carter family, including a Jacob, emigrated to Bertie County, North Carolina, as early as 1720. According to several researchers this was the same Jacob Carter who moved on to Colleton County, South Carolina, where he received a royal land grant in 1747. He settled down and lived in Colleton on the Little Saltketchie River there.

There is a deed of gift found in records in Charleston, South Carolina, dated April 7, 1787, from Jacob Carter to his son, George Carter, for a tract of fifty acres on Little Swamp on the east side of the Little Saltketchie which had previously been granted to the elder Carter. Both father and son were identified in the deed as residents of St. Bartholomew's Parrish, Colleton County. This solidifies the family relationship between George and Jacob, father and son.

George Carter

George, the third son of Jacob Carter, was born around 1740, probably in South Carolina. He married in 1772 but the name of his wife is unknown. Judge Huxford wrote a long profile of him in Volume 3 of *Pioneers of Wiregrass Georgia* in which he stated that George served in the Cherokee Expedition of 1759-1760, thus confirming his presence in the state by then. Huxford then stated that George was a Revolutionary soldier in South Carolina but that the details of his service have not been learned. Later discoveries show that George enlisted on February 5, 1778, in the 3rd South Carolina Regiment, Capt. John Carraway Smith's 9th Company of the Continental Line, until the expiration of his service on July 1, 1779. His total pay during that time was $192.44. Since there were no other George Carters in South Carolina serving in the Continental Army at that time there is little doubt that this is our

George Carter in spite of that common name. The DAR has also accepted this service record. During that period of his service his unit fought at the Battle of Stono, a significant battle. It was also at the Battle of Charleston in 1780 where his unit was captured, as were the other Continental soldiers there. It is not known whether George was present at those two battles.

George moved with his father and brothers to Tattnall County, Georgia, in about 1808 where he purchased 575 acres of land along the Ohoopee River in January 1809 from Samuel Parrish, and, later that year, another adjoining 575 acre tract from Phillip Griner. Two years later the State granted him a 1,000 acre tract which was also along the Ohoopee. In 1819 when Appling County, which abutted Tattnall, opened up for settlement, most of George's sons moved there. The 1820 Census shows that he was living in Tattnall but appears listed as a resident of Appling in the Land Lottery of that year, being listed as George Carter, Sr. His death occurred some two years later when he was over eighty. His wife's date of death is not known, nor is the burial site for either.

Children of George Carter and wife (unknown)

1. **Jesse, b. 1774; d. 1847; m. Molsy Touchton.**
2. Sarah, b. 1776; d.1863; m. Isaac Moody.
3. George, b. 1782; d. unk; Elizabeth Baxter on Feb 4, 1807.
4. David, b. 1785; d. 1825; m. Rachel Cooper.
5. Mary, b. 1787; d.1846; m. Samuel E. Swilley on Feb 27, 1817.
6. Jacob, b. 1789; d. unk; m. Jerusha Beverly.
7. Isaac, b. 1790; d. 1854; m. Ellender _____.
8. Jane, b. 1792; d. unk; m. Drew Reddish.

9. Rebecca, b. 1794; d. unk; m. Stephen Baxter.

10. William, b. 1795; d. 1855; m. Margaret Durrance (?)

Jesse Carter

Most often referred to as Captain Jesse as a result of his leadership during the Indian war of the 1830's, he was born in Colleton County, South Carolina, in 1774, the son of George Carter. He married Mary "Molsy" Touchton there in about 1798. Her parents are not known. As noted in the previous profile Jesse moved with his father, brothers and other relatives to Tattnall County, Georgia, shortly after that county was created in the early 1800s. In August 1809 Jesse surveyed 199 acres on Watermelon Creek in Tattnall and in October in the same year, another 631 acres adjoining his first purchase. Records show that he sold both properties when he moved away.

When Appling was created and opened up to settlers in 1819, Jesse, along with other members of his extended family, moved across the Altamaha River into the new county. He acquired land about six miles southeast of old Holmesville, the ante-bellum county seat. The first term of the Appling County Superior Court was held at his home in 1820 as well as the first county election. He was elected one of the first county justices of the inferior court and he served until the following election. The Georgia State Legislature appointed him in November 1822 as "one of the Commissioners to select a site for the public building in and for County of Appling."

One of the main reasons for the Carter family's frequent moves was to find better pasturage for their heads of cattle. When, in

1825, Jesse sold all his property in Appling, he relocated on the west side of the Alapaha River in Lowndes County, Georgia, which had been opened up for settlement just the previous year. It is said that Jesse brought with him on that move some 1,260 head of cattle which were tended to by his sons William and George and several slaves. That is a lot of cattle, and he also must have had other animals as well.

Jesse built a large plantation home on his newly purchased land located about one and one-half miles south of the present town of Lakeland, now in Lanier County. In 1825 he donated a piece of that land for a "meeting house" on the banks of the Alapaha River and a few months later the Union Primitive Baptist Church, the first church in Lowndes County, was organized there. Although he gave the land and built the original building almost single-handedly, he does not appear in the church records to have become a member. His wife was a member and was baptized into the church in December 1827. She died a member of this church.

The Union Baptist Church later burned but was rebuilt in 1854. A wooden church, it has been renovated several times over the years but never to a really good condition. Because it had deteriorated, it ceased to function as a church. Over the decades the building had even begun to tilt towards the Alapaha River and was nearly a foot and a half off center. In the late 1990s with the help of a local development grant and some expert carpentry the building was completely restored. It is now owned by Lanier County and can be used for family reunions and other such occasions.

Jesse became only the second Representative from Lowndes County in the State Legislature, serving one term in 1827. He raised a militia company during the Indian War of 1838 and served as its captain from July 1 to October 15, 1838. He resigned his captaincy owing to his age—he was fifty eight—and turned his command over to a younger man to lead the troops he raised into battle with the Indians.

Jesse died in 1847 at the age of seventy three. The Lowndes County appraisement book for the period 1846-1854, the only county record book that survived the 1870 courthouse fire, contained Jesse's estate inventory as of September 8, 1847, which indicates that he had probably died earlier that year. But it also lists his assets. He then owned 184 head of cattle, eight slaves, and Land Lots numbers 413, 414, 415, 416 and 516 in the 11th District of the original Irwin County, now Lowndes. The slaves were sold at public auction on January 5, 1848, by the estate administrators, William and George, his sons. The land was sold on January 2, 1849, also by auction. In both of these sales, the slaves and cattle were purchased by some of his heirs. His home became the property of his youngest daughter, Nancy Carter Darsey, and she and her mother continued to make it their home until Mary's death sometime around 1858.

Jesse and Mary are buried in the Union Primitive Baptist Church Cemetery which is just across the road from the church. Both are located on Burnt Church road, south of Lakeland off state highway 135.

Children of Jesse Carter and Mary (Molsy) Touchton

1. William, b. 1801; d. 1852; m. Nannie Monk in 1823.
2. George, b. 1805; d. 1860; m. Mary Parrish.

3. Rachel, b. Aug 6, 1806; d. Dec 28, 1874; m. William Cone Knight in 1826.

4. James, b. 1809; d. 1883; m. Pollie Bennett in 1830. Both James and John below are given the birth date of 1809 in Pioneers of Wiregrass Georgia. A typo, or are they twins?

5. John, b. 1809; d. 1864; m. Elizabeth Knight.

6. **Sarah, b. 1815; d. 1850; m. Dennis Wetherington in 1830.**

7. Isaac, b. 1816; d. 1853; m. Rachel Sirmons in 1842.

8. Elijah, b. Jun 8, 1821; d. Dec 20, 1908, m. Nicy Prescott.

9. Nancy, b. Jun 26, 1825; d. Feb 27, 1881; m. James Anders Darsey on Jan 25, 1846.

The Horne Lineage

Nothing is known about our Horne ancestry other than the belief that Thomas Horne had originally emigrated from Ulster, Ireland, to the British colonies in America sometime prior to the Revolutionary War.

Thomas Horne

Thomas was born about 1740 in Ulster, Ireland, and came to the colonies before the Revolutionary War. He eventually settled along Flat Creek in the northeastern part of Darlington County, South Carolina. He married Elizabeth before 1764, and they had at least two children. His military service during the Revolutionary War is well known as a result of five letters he wrote to his wife during the war. He enlisted in the 3rd South Carolina Regiment under Colonel William Thomson on July 24, 1776, (apparently the paperwork took place after the battle was over), and official records show that he served for a time in Capt. Felix Warley's Company.

Thomas was present at the Battle of Sullivan Island, South Carolina, on June 28, 1776, an important battle in that it kept Charleston in the hands of the Continental Army until 1780. His regimental unit helped defend the Breach Inlet, which protected the rear of Ft. Moultrie, which, in turn, protected Charleston harbor. During their attack that day on Thomson's forces, the British were thoroughly defeated and retreated back to their ships. One historical account states that Col. Thomson's soldiers were old Indian fighters; evidently they knew how to fight.

Two of the five letters he mailed home over a two-year period contain his comments on this battle. In 1778 he was serving once again in the militia, and in at least one of those letters, he mentioned his participation in the East Florida military campaign that took place in March through May of 1778. In several of them he complains about his poor health, and, in fact, begs his wife to try to find a substitute for him so that he could come home to recover and be with his family. Sometime in late 1778, after writing his last letter, dated September 10, 1778, Thomas died, probably succumbing to his illnesses. These five letters are copied in Appendix "A" of this book.

His wife, Elizabeth Foxworth Horne, also assisted the Revolutionary War efforts by supplying provisions to the Continental Army. On June 10, 1782, she was paid for selling 250 pounds of beef for use by the Georgetown, South Carolina, garrison that year. Meta Shaw Coleman joined the DAR by tracing her lineage to Patriot Elizabeth Horne. Elizabeth received a pension for his military service with the first payment being made on October 16, 1792. Her son Richard witnessed at least one of those payments. The last payment made to her was on August 15, 1803, indicating that she must have died shortly thereafter. It is believed that she was living with her son Richard in Beaufort District, South Carolina, at the time of her death.

Children of Thomas Horne and Elizabeth (unknown)

1. **Richard, b. Feb 11, 1764; d. Jan 10, 1840; m. 1st unk and 2nd Mary Gordon Hendley.**

2. Sally, no further information.

Richard Horne

Richard was probably born in 1764 in Darlington County, South Carolina, the son of Thomas and Elizabeth Horne. He married twice although the name of his first wife is unknown. He appears in the 1800 census for Beaufort District with a wife between twenty six and forty five years of age and three daughters under ten, about whom nothing else is known. In the 1810 census for that district, he had a wife and four daughters under sixteen. The additional daughter was Rachel, born to Richard and his second wife, Mary Hendley Gordon. It is apparent that his first wife had died after 1800, leaving him alone with their three daughters. He had married Mary after his first wife's death but before the birth of Rachel in 1808.

Mary was a widow with three children of her own whose names were William, Jerusha and Suzanne Gordon although this has not been confirmed. Richard and Mary Hendley then produced at least three children of their own: Rachel, born in 1808, as noted; Hendley, born 1814; and a third daughter whose name is unknown and who probably died young. Their son Hendley, interviewed for his profile in the *Memoirs of Georgia*, published in 1895, was quoted as follows: "Mr. [Hendley] Horne was the youngest of three children born to his father by his second and last marriage." It's complicated.

Richard served as a soldier during the Revolutionary War; however, details of his military service are not known. Nevertheless, he was awarded two land grants in the 1820 Georgia Land Lottery for his military service. The *Authentic List of Land Grants to Veterans of the Revolutionary War* confirms his service, but it is the only source to do so. Perhaps he served in the militia in South Carolina during the 1780/81 period when a lot of fighting was going on there and the records of soldiers doing the fighting were not well kept. He was only sixteen or seventeen then but it was not uncommon in those days for boys of that age to wield a weapon. Anyway, he provided the authorities with sufficient evidence to warrant his eligibility for land grants for his military service.

Sometime after the war ended, Richard and his family, including his widowed mother, moved to Beaufort District, south of Charleston, where, in 1815, the state granted him 1,000 acres on Saltketchers Swamp for his service in Lt. Col. John Ashe Alston's South Carolina Militia Regiment during the War of 1812. He lived there with his wife, Mary, until about 1817 when he moved to

Georgia. Apparently he first settled in McIntosh County, where he registered for the above two land grants for his military service. Sometime later he moved next door to Liberty County, now Long County, where he lived the rest of his life in the Jones Creek community. Mary joined the Jones Creek Baptist Church on April 24, 1823, while Richard was baptized on that same day.

Mary Horne died on November 1, 1832, at the age of fifty; Richard on January 10, 1840 at the age of seventy six. Both are buried in the Jones Creek Baptist Church Cemetery which is located about five miles north of Ludowici, Long County, on US 301. Both the old and the new church are on the left side of the highway. Their grave markers can still be seen.

Children of Richard Horne and first wife (unknown) and second wife, Mary Hendley Gordon

1. **Rachel**, b. Mar 13, 1808; d. Nov 8, 1877; m. **Jeremiah Shaw, Jr.**

2. Hendley Foxworth, b. Jan 19, 1814; d. Jan 17, 1899; m. 1st Anna S. Parker on Oct 1, 1831, 2nd Sarah Mary Smiley on Dec 18, 1841, and 3rd Sarah Long on Jan 22, 1857. Hendley joined the Georgia Militia during the Civil War and fought at the Battle of Good Hope Church near Marietta, Georgia. He was wounded there, but afterwards walked to Macon, purchased a small boat and floated down the Altamaha River to their nearby home. He designed and built the wooden Jones Creek Baptist Church which was occupied from 1856 until 1958 when it was replaced by a brick church. The old church is still standing and is now being used for meetings and family get-togethers. Hendley also served as a judge

of the inferior court, a justice of the peace and a Georgia state representative.

Photographs

Jeremiah and Elizabeth Holland Coleman, c. 1880

Daniel Wade Coleman, c. 1900

Daniel Ernest Coleman wearing his Fez, 1949

Nancy Hendley Hargrove, wife of A. J. Hargrove, c. 1920

Nancy Hendley Hargrove, aged 96, with son Larkin Hargrove

Larkin Llmore and Elizabeth Hamilton Hargrove, c. 1925

Alice Hargrove Coleman with grandsons Wade and Dan Coleman, c. 1944

William Jasper and Elizabeth Wetherington Shaw, c. 1890

Meta Charles Shaw in her wedding dress, 1909

Shaw home at 1115
N. Patterson Street
in Valdosta

Lowndes Walton Shaw in his
Vedette uniform, c. 1887

Lowndes Walton Shaw and
Meta Aubrey Charles Shaw, c. 1930

Mary Crews Charles, c. 1870

Callie Daughtrey Charles, c. 1920

Garret Vinzant Charles, c. 1895

Virginia and Meta Shaw, c. 1921

Meta Shaw and Theo Coleman's wedding, 1938

(L-R) Hargrove Coleman with his younger
brother, Theo, c. 1955

Pfc. Theo Coleman at Sloppy
Joe's Bar in Havana, Cuba,
1945

Theo, Meta, Dan and Wade Coleman,
1944

Meta Coleman and her five
sons, l-r, Richard, Stephen,
John, Dan and Wade, c. 1980

Meta Shaw (center) with unidentified shipmates on the *M.V. Saturnia* prior to sailing from New York City to Europe. Summer of 1937.

(L-R) Virginia Shaw Girardin and Meta Shaw Coleman, sisters

Engagement Party for Dan and Carolyn, November 6, 2009. (L-R) Wade and Geri Coleman, Richard and Robin Coleman, Sharon and Buddy Coleman, Kay and Stephen Coleman, Frank Kelly (Dan's close friend from Peace Corps days), Grant and Ginger Eager, Allen Eager. Dan and Carolyn sitting on sofa.

Dan and Carolyn Coleman, 2011

Chapter 4

Florida Territory
The Charles Family

Family Tree for
Meta Aubrey Charles: Florida Territory
4 Generations

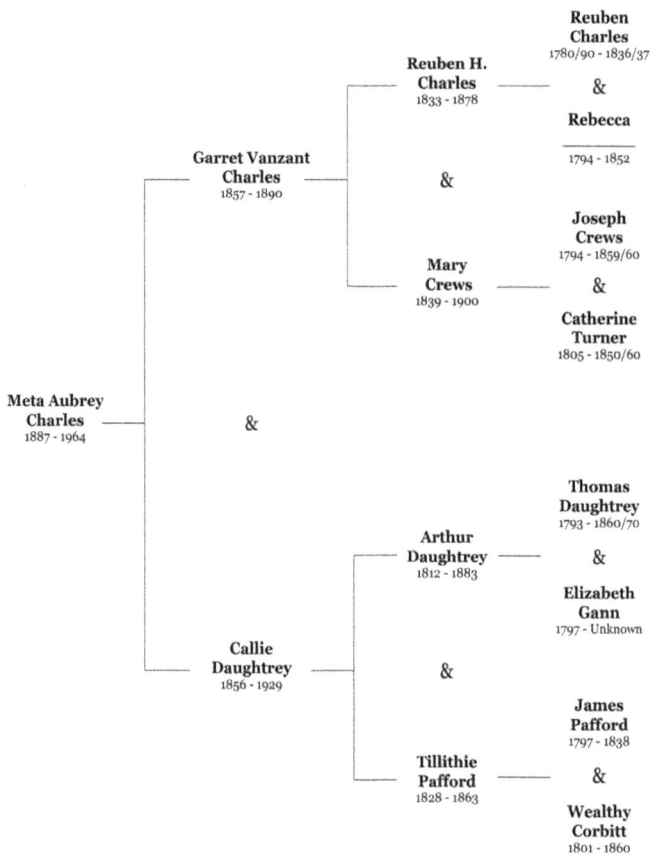

Reuben Charles
1780/90 - 1836/37

Reuben H. Charles
1833 - 1878

&

Rebecca

1794 - 1852

Garret Vanzant Charles
1857 - 1890

&

Joseph Crews
1794 - 1859/60

Mary Crews
1839 - 1900

&

Catherine Turner
1805 - 1850/60

Meta Aubrey Charles
1887 - 1964

&

Thomas Daughtrey
1793 - 1860/70

Arthur Daughtrey
1812 - 1883

&

Elizabeth Gann
1797 - Unknown

Callie Daughtrey
1856 - 1929

&

James Pafford
1797 - 1838

Tillithie Pafford
1828 - 1863

&

Wealthy Corbitt
1801 - 1860

Chapter 4

Florida Territory
The Charles Family

The territory of Florida was, with a few exceptions, mostly populated in its early days in the northern part along the Georgia border. As Georgia expanded, more and more settlers crossed over the border, while others took advantage of the growth of the St. Augustine area to arrive via the sea. Our ancestors not only arrived in Florida by those two routes but, after the state joined the Union and began to grow, they came from other Southern states, including directly from Tennessee. Like today, they saw it as a land of opportunity. With its three hundred plus years of mostly

Spanish rule its culture then, and even now, seems somewhat unique, maybe not even southern. Our ancestors, particularly the Charles lineage, did not follow the most common career of farming. Instead they were pioneer merchants with all the diverse interests that merchants, but not farmers, usually have. The other lineages—Daughtrey, Crews and Pafford—are here as well, most of whom were farmers.

The Charles Lineage

There is no question but that Reuben Charles is our first documented ancestor in this line. And there is strong circumstantial evidence that Andrew Charles of Charleston, South Carolina, was his father. According to Andrew's obituary in the *Charleston Times* of April 25, 1812, "Died, on the 25th inst., in the 47th year of his age. Mr. Andrew Charles, a native of Pennsylvania, and for upwards of 20 years, a respectable Merchant of this city." We know from this obituary when he was born—about 1765—and where, how long he lived in Charleston and what he did for a living. The 1790 US Census in Pennsylvania listed an Andrew Charles, the only one enumerated in the entire United States, living in Berks County, and that he had a wife and two sons younger than ten years of age, meaning the two boys were born between 1780 and 1790. By the 1800 US census, Andrew Charles was not living in Pennsylvania but there was an Andrew Charles in Charleston then with a wife and two sons over ten years of age, all of which confirms the obituary information that these two Charles' were one and the same.

But there is some confusion. The 1810 Census for Charleston shows Andrew with seven children: one son and two daughters under ten years and two sons and two daughters between ten and sixteen years. It is likely that some of these children, particularly the children under ten, could have been children born to them between 1800 and 1810, but what about the two boys under sixteen? It is unlikely those two boys could be the same two boys born before 1790 in Pennsylvania, but where were they during the previous census period of 1800 and 1810? Was there a second wife? Were they adopted children or apprentices? Who knows? The obituary mentions only that he left behind seven children and his wife.

The *Charleston City Directory*, published periodically since 1784, provides the name, address and profession of every city head of household. Andrew first appears in 1794 as a grocer living at 130 Broad Street. Then by 1801 he had become a merchant with his home identified as 16 Liberty Street. By 1809 he is a merchant in the firm of Hopkins and Charles on Vanderhorst's Wharf, with his home address given as 10 Eliott Street, a house that is still standing. Newspaper records and advertisements of the period indicate that Hopkins and Charles was a substantial trading business with its own schooners importing goods for sale.

Andrew's long obituary is informative in some ways, but it did not mention a single family member. His very short will did not mention his family either, yet it listed twelve men as his potential executors. Nearly all are designated as merchants, chandlers, planters or similar, in short, important men in the Charleston community. The will was proved on May 15, 1812, and two of these men, Thomas Blackwood and Robert Maxwell, both merchants, were selected as executors. There was an inventory of his estate that showed that he owned a well-furnished home and two slaves, probably for house purposes. Probate records that might indicate how the estate was distributed among family members were likely destroyed during the Civil War fires. To date not a single record has been found to indicate the names of Andrew's family.

Based on the above information about Andrew and the known facts about Reuben Charles, it is reasonable to assume that they were father and son. By profession both were merchants. Reuben was a ship captain while his father owned schooners and hired others to sail them. Reuben named this first son, Andrew Jackson Charles, which implies that he could have named him for his father as well as the Hero of the Battle of New Orleans. Reuben's oldest son was born in South Carolina in 1815 where he, Reuben, was placed at about the same time, signing a promissory note with a Charleston factor the following year. All these facts show that Reuben had a strong Charleston connection. Two of Andrew's sons were born between 1780 and 1790 while Reuben declares in the 1830 Florida census that he was born during that same time period.

Incidentally, in the 1819 Charleston directory, a Sarah Charles, widow, is living at 16 Cummings Street. She also appears in the 1820 census but not in the 1830 census. The *Abstract of Wills, Charleston District*, states that, "Andrew Charles is the Executor of John Minnick, who died on 11 August 1795; he is the brother-in-law of John Minnick." So could we surmise that the given name of Andrew's wife was Sarah and that her maiden name Minnick? Maybe.

Reuben Charles

Reuben was probably born in Berks County, Pennsylvania, between 1780 and 1790, the son of Andrew Charles, as purported. If Andrew, born 1765, was his father, then Reuben and his brother were actually born after 1785 when Andrew was twenty but before 1790, the date of the census. Reuben moved with his family to Charleston, South Carolina, in the early 1790s where his father became a successful merchant. Reuben made his living initially as a trader along the Southeastern Atlantic sea routes. Records show that he owned and/or captained several schooners, hence the bestowal of the honorific of captain as he was referred to by many for the rest of his life. There is no record of his ever serving in a military unit.

In March 1816 Reuben was in Charleston, where he signed a promissory note for $800 made out to H. P. Dawes, a factor. In the following year John Litchfield repaid Reuben for an undetermined debt. In 1818 he paid $1.56 in state and county taxes to James Eppings, Collector of Customs in Savannah, and, as well, purchased two horses from Abel Gibbs there. Frances Watts signed an IOU made out to Reuben in Savannah dated February of that same year. All of this indicates that his business involved travel in those coastal cities.

He was in St. Augustine as early as 1815 when he acquired goods for his schooner, *William*. Two years later in this same city he provisioned *Norwich*, another schooner he captained. In May of 1819 Reuben petitioned the Spanish Governor of St. Augustine to let him sell a twenty foot long three-decker boat by the name of *Maria Francesa,* but the petition was denied. In this same petition he claims St. Augustine residency which is his first known home as an adult.

In 1821, after the Spaniards left Florida, the U. S. Congress appointed a commission to validate the ownership of land granted during Spanish rule, and Reuben proceeded to lay claim to two pieces of land he had settled on in the St. Augustine area. The largest tract contained 640 acres in Township 5, and was located about a dozen miles from the city near Twelve Mile Swamp. At the claim enquiry several witnesses swore that Reuben had settled on the tract of land as early as 1817, had built one or more houses, and was growing crops and raising cattle there. A neighbor, George Gianopoly, swore in August 1825 that "he [Reuben Charles] was on the land claimed by Reuben Charles in November 1818 and it was considered as public land. Claimant built a large log house on said land and had three or four acres of land cleared and was clearing land in 1818. That in the year 1819 he planted the said cleared land in rice and corn and that he continued in possession of said land until August 1824." The commission approved his claim but for only 350 acres.

The second tract consisted of one hundred acres he had settled on near Nine Mile Spring on Kings Road in Township 6 which was also confirmed. In his memorial (petition) regarding this tract, Reuben stated that, "Luis Schofield took possession and cultivated it; some time after which he absconded with a woman, not his wife, leaving his family; that his wife Margaret Schofield on the 2nd day of June 1823 sold the said property to this Claimant." The Governor of Spanish Florida, Tomas de Aguilar, had granted this land to Schofield in June 1796.

On September 23, 1823, Reuben signed a contract with Moses Elias Levy to manage Pilgrimage Plantation which consisted of about 20,000 acres (perhaps as much as 38,800 acres per another account later) of the much larger Arredondo land grant of 289,645 acres, as one survey showed, all of which lay in present day Alachua County, and was then owned by Fernando de la Maza Arredondo, a former citizen of Spanish Florida. Arredondo had received this grant in 1817 from the King of Spain with the stipulation that he settle the land with two-hundred families, a stipulation which Arredondo found difficult to achieve. After Florida became a U.S. territory, Arredondo made an arrangement with Levy, one of the most important and influential men in this lightly populated territory, to bring in settlers and thereby, it was hoped, to ensure that his grant would be validated by the new government. Levy had vast holdings in the area that later become Levy County, Florida, and his son, David Levy Yulee, became the first U. S. Senator from Florida after the state joined the union. Yulee was also the first Jewish United States Senator although he had converted to Christianity by that time and had taken his mother's maiden name which did not sound very Jewish.

Throughout Reuben's tenure as Pilgrimage Plantation's manager, he corresponded frequently with Levy and his agent in St. Augustine, Davis Floyd, a lawyer, about the management and operation of the plantation. On October 23, 1826, a little over three years since Reuben had signed on as manager, Floyd wrote to him that Levy had decided to make other arrangements for managing the plantation and that his contract would not be renewed. This correspondence and many other documents and papers involving Reuben's activities between about 1815 and 1836 were preserved and are now located in the Department of Special Collections of the University of Florida library. They are identified as the Reuben Charles Papers but also known as the Virginia Shaw Girardin and Meta Shaw Coleman Collection. His descendants donated these papers to the university in 1998, and since then a number of writers and researchers have accessed them. See Attachment "B" for a sample plus more information.

On April 14, 1824, while Reuben was still managing the plantation, Moses Levy and Joseph Arredando, a son of Fernando Arredondo, asked him to undertake a survey of the 58,400 acre tract they owned near Alligator Town "on both sides of [Alligator] Creek [extending] 2 and ½ miles on each bank and running from its head 19 miles." In 1830 Reuben was called to testify before the East Florida Superior Court hearing Levy's claim for the Alligator Tract. By this time the size of this tract was revealed to be a paltry 38,000 acres all of which was located in the future Columbia County. Reuben stated to the court that he had been unable to locate any such Alligator Creek although he "knows the country well having been over it frequently" and that Alligator town, which today is Lake City, "consisted of an old field and a number of houses in ruins, Indian huts not inhabited." The Superior Count approved the claim which was upheld in 1839 by the U.S. Supreme Court.

In 1824 the Territorial Council granted Rueben a charter to operate a trading post and ferry where the Bellamy Trail would later cross the Suwannee River in Columbia County, now Suwannee County. This trail was hacked out of the woods by John Bellamy under contract to the Council, and connected East Florida from St. Augustine through to Tallahassee. It generally followed the former Spanish Trail which had been in disrepair since the Spanish left. Reuben and other landowners affected by the trail signed a certificate to the Governor's agent that the road "has been executed properly and substantially and the road opened in such a manner as will be satisfactory to the Government."

In February 1830 John Bellamy's son Abraham crossed the river on the Charles Ferry where he was billed a total of $8.12 ½ for two wagons to use the ferry, plus lodging and two meals for four people at the Charles' trading post there. Operating a river ferry, trading post and inn in Florida's interior at that time may have been profitable, but it was not without its dangers. On Dec, 1825, Delegate Joseph M. White, who represented the Territory in the U.S. House of Representatives read on the House floor a petition from Reuben which stated that "He had established a ferry on the Suwannee at great expense and had suffered depredations by the Indians and praying for the grant of a small tract on each side of the River."

In March 1826 and again in 1827 Reuben was named an Alachua County justice of the peace. He was appointed the postmaster of Wanton in 1826 (this may have been after he left the job of plantation manager) and as a requirement for the job he had to post a $300 bond. Reuben signed an agreement in January 1827 with George Downs for the latter to sharecrop a plantation he had recently leased from Thomas Brush. In December 1828 Reuben agreed to sell and deliver to Owen March $290 worth of beef by the end of next April. On July 10, 1829, President Andrew Jackson signed a deed granting Reuben eighty acres of public land in Township 4, Range 11, near St. Augustine which he had already purchased.

Reuben Charles was many things in life: merchant, trader, farmer, plantation manager, innkeeper, ferryman, postmaster, justice of the peace and ship captain. He was also a family man, having married Rebecca sometime before 1815, and whose maiden name and origins are completely unknown. We do know her date of birth, April 30, 1794, which was calculated based on information on her marker. They had at least four children over a span of eighteen years, indicating that they had probably had other children who did not survive owing to the unhealthy Florida climate. Their first child was born in South Carolina while the other three in Florida.

As a pioneer in North Central Florida Reuben and his family lived an arduous and isolated existence. In his account of his travails in the 2nd Seminole War, J. R. Motte writes that ". . .we proceeded down the east bank of the Suwannee towards Charles Ferry, where we designed striking on the main road to Newmansville. We encamped for one night near Charles Ferry, and renewed at an early hour next morning our weary march. We were apparently the first to travel over this route with wheels since the war commenced; and a slow and tedious time we had; stopping every five minutes to clear away fallen trees which blocked the road; sinking through the soft spongy ground if we deserted the beaten track to circumvent the obstructions. We found great scarcity of water also upon the route and suffered much from thirst."

During the Second Seminole War, Charles Ferry was a rendezvous point for military units. For example, men from Livingston's Mounted Volunteers of Madison County met at Charles Ferry to organize the unit and assembled there whenever the unit was called together to repel Seminoles coming into the area to raid and pillage. The family probably remained at their home on the bluff above the ferry landing during the war years since, of course, the military needed the ferry. One account indicates that there was even a small fort at Charles Ferry which would have permitted the family to remain there in relative safety.

But it was not to be. Sometime after 1836 Reuben was killed. The story passed down is that one day he and another man were walking along the Suwannee River when they were killed by a band of Indians hiding out on the other side of the river. After his death Rebecca continued to run the ferry and operate the trading post while rearing her three children still at home. In 1840 Florida's Legislative Council granted her the right to continue to operate the ferry in her deceased husband's place. From existing records it is estimated that she owned around 1,000 acres of land on both sides of the river, that is, in both Madison and Columbia Counties. Columbia County tax records show that she owned twelve slaves in 1845, which had increased to sixteen by 1850.

Her death illustrates the dangers of those pioneer times. Despite the circumstances of her husband's death it appears that she still managed to maintain friendly relations with the Indians living nearby. It is said that she always wore a red bandana or headband so that whenever she left her home place the Indians would recognize her as someone they knew and trusted. One day she forgot to wear this bandana when she walked down to the spring to fetch some water. A passing Indian, probably a member of the Miccosukee tribe, and not recognizing her without the bandana, shot and killed her. It was an accident, said the Indians, and they were sorry it happened. An alternative legend claims that she was shot while standing on her porch, and that Mary was killed by the Indians when she went to fetch water. Since we know that Mary was still alive in 1866, I tend to disregard this second story.

Both Reuben and Rebecca are buried on a plot of land that appears to be an Indian mound about one-hundred yards upland from Charles Spring. There are indications of at least four other gravesites there but only Rebecca's is marked. Its survival as a family cemetery has been and will continue to be problematic. Virginia Shaw Girardin remembered visiting it sometime before WWII and saw what she says was both Reuben's and Rebecca's grave stones and that there was an iron fence surrounding the site. When her son, David, visited the site in 1976 he saw only Rebecca's upright headstone, and the fence had disappeared. By 1983 the upright headstone had been knocked over and broken; however, the county authorities re-assembled it by placing it flat on the ground with cement to hold the broken pieces together. It was soon forgotten and bushes and weeds took over the cemetery.

In early 1999 I asked Jinnie Hancock at the Suwannee Valley Genealogical Society to help me relocate the grave site. She contacted Bivian Howell who lived nearby and had remembered seeing it often many years earlier. Bivian, her husband, Murl, and another neighbor, Jim Butler, who was also a part-Cherokee Indian, immediately began to search once again for it. After locating it they cleared all the old growth and hacked out a clear path to it. Later, with my twelve-year-old nephew, Rick Coleman, in tow, we met up with the Howells, Butler and several members of the genealogical society for a site visit. To our surprise, once we got there, Jim Butler staged a ceremony in which he, as an Indian representing all Indians, asked us, Rebecca's descendants, to forgive the Indians for having killed her. At the end of the ceremony Jim asked our group of about ten people to gather in a circle around her grave and hold hands, and for the youngest person there to say a prayer. Rick was the youngest but even at that age he was not at a loss for words. He said, "I pray that the Indian and the white man will live in peace. We forgive the Indians for killing Rebecca." No other person there or, anywhere else for that matter, could have uttered a more appropriate prayer.

On Sunday, November 4, 2001, the Abraham Venable Chapter of the Florida Society, Colonial Dames of the Seventeenth Century placed a historical marker at the Charles Family Cemetery. More than two-hundred people attended the dedication ceremony that day, including many members of Colonial Dames, the Suwannee Valley Genealogical Society, county commissioners, merely interested folks and several Charles descendants, including their third great grandsons, Jerry and David Girardin and Dan, John and Richard Coleman, and some of their children. We, her descendants, placed flowers on Rebecca's gravestone.

A couple of years ago someone bought the tract of land on which the cemetery lies. The new owners have erected a substantial fence with a gate around the cemetery section. Normally, the gate is left unlocked, and visitors are able to visit the site freely. The cemetery's GPS coordinates are N30.16524 W083.22885.

On Rebecca's marble headstone is engraved a willow tree with the following text: "Sacred to the Memory of Rebecca Charles, who departed this life January 25, 1852, aged 57 years, 8 months and 25 days". A prayer then reads:

In hope I rest beneath the ground,

Though mingled with the dust;

Yet when the angels trump shall sound,

Will rise in Christ I trust.

Thou are laid in the grave, we no longer behold thee,

Nor thread the rough paths of this world by thy side;

But the wide arms of mercy are spread to enfold thee,

And sinners pray hope since the Savior hath died.

Children of Reuben Charles and Rebecca (unknown)

1. Andrew Jackson, b. 1815; d. unk; m. Delana Rosella Townsend in Mar 1841. The 1850 census shows Andrew and his family living in Madison County, Florida, however they are nowhere found in any 1860 census. But their three children, Emily, Fannie and Rupert, were living at that time with Andrew's sister, Drucilla, in New River (Bradford) County. Nothing else is known of Andrew and Delana. Rupert served with his uncle in the Civil War, was

left sick in Kentucky after the Battle of Perryville, and shows up in Wakulla, Florida, in 1870, working for the Customs Office. A list of Lake City's police chiefs—constables in those early days—shows that Rupert served in that position from 1880 to 1885. After that, nothing is known of him. Fannie married Matthew Scarborough and their daughter, Ruby, married Fred Cone.

Governor Fred Cone

Reuben Charles' son, Andrew Jackson Charles, had a daughter named Francis ("Fannie") who married Matthew Scarborough. Their daughter, Ruby, married a lawyer and politician from Lake City named Fred Cone. Unfortunately, Ruby died in 1923, which was thirteen years before Fred, by then remarried, was elected Florida's Governor to a four-year term beginning in 1936. Thus, Ruby never came to be known as Florida's first lady. Virginia Shaw Girardin remembered, as a child, visiting her grandmother, Callie Charles, in Lake City and going with her cousins for a wild ride in Fred's big convertible all over the city. It was really fun, she said, and Fred was a fine man.

---

2. Drucilla, b. Aug 26, 1823; d. Mar 6, 1866; m. 1st Thomas Hughes Hines on Mar 12, 1852, and 2nd Milbern L. Odom on Apr 17, 1859. She had three children with her two husbands. She died in Suwannee County where her sister, Mary, was the executor of her estate, per records there.

3. Mary, b. 1828; d. after 1866; m. William T. McLeran on Jan 29, 1860. Mary is recorded alone in the 1860 Florida census with only her daughter, Fannie. William died on May 29, 1860, only four months after his marriage, and is buried at Little River Cemetery in Suwannee County. Mary was named his estate executor. Except for her role as her sister's estate executor, nothing more has been heard of either Mary or Fannie.

4. **Reuben Henry, b. 1833; d. Apr 11, 1878; married Mary Crews in 1851.**

Reuben Henry Charles

Reuben Henry, so as to distinguish him from his father, was almost certainly born at Charles Spring in Columbia County, Florida, in 1833, just before his father died a couple of years later. The Second Seminole War began two years after his birth, meaning that he spent most of his early years living in a war environment. Around the time his mother died in 1852, he moved to Lake City, the Columbia County seat. There, he worked as a merchant, as his father and grandfather had done. Along the way he met and married Mary Crews, the daughter of Joseph and Catherine Crews, originally of Jacksonville, and who may have moved to Lake City before her marriage. Reuben Henry and Mary had only one child, Garret, who was named after his father's friend and neighbor, Garret Vinzant, whose wife was Julia Goodbread Vinzant. Julia was the daughter of John and Charity Crews Goodbread, while Charity was the sister of Joseph Crews, the father of Mary Crews. If you get that relationship, then you are a genealogist. But it shows how some folks wind up getting married.

Reuben Henry's first military experience came when he was in his early twenties. He served as a 2nd Sergeant in Capt. A. J. Wright's Mounted Detachment during the Third (and last) Seminole War. He was mustered into that unit in April 1856 and served until the unit was dissolved shortly thereafter. Records then show that he was a private in Capt. Wright's Special Battalion of Florida Volunteers from May 18, 1856, until September 30, 1856. It is likely that the first unit was merged into the second since they were both volunteer units under the same company commander. He served a total of five months in this war.

In 1859 he was appointed to serve as the Captain of Columbia County's 1st Militia Company which was founded in anticipation of an expected "slave uprising." In 1860 the Governor of Florida called for, and the State Legislature authorized, the establishment of militia companies to prepare for any possible military action against the states opposed to Southern secession. Reuben Henry was again appointed Captain of the 1st Militia Company in Lake City and served in that position until the Civil War began and he resigned to join up with a regular Confederate unit.

With the outbreak of war Reuben Henry enlisted on October 3, 1861, in Company "A", 1st Regiment of Florida Cavalry. He was elected a 1st Lieutenant in this company which was composed almost entirely of men from the Lake City area. One pay record shows he was paid through April 30, 1862, although at a later unknown date he resigned or was discharged. Because his election as lieutenant was for six months, he may not have been re-elected. Regardless, on March 26 1863, he enlisted in Company "C", 1st Battalion (Brevard's) Florida Partisan Rangers, but the records show that he was "detailed to arrest deserters" or "detailed to enroll conscripts," depending on which monthly voucher one scans. He was wounded in 1864 while chasing deserters and discharged for health reasons.

He had joined Brevard's battalion as a private and left a private, but it appears he was anything but a regular soldier. Instead he was like a policeman, out on his own, to make sure that soldiers were available to fight. Desertion was a major problem in the South as the war progressed, seemingly an unending one. In one instance it was a woman who was caught up in the war. One voucher shows that he was reimbursed $138 for detaining a certain Miss Mary Tyler at his home. The date is September 10, 1864, and the voucher explains that "This lady was ordered by Gen. Anderson to be held in Lake City under surveillance." Major H. S. Routh authorized payment after which Reuben Henry acknowledged said receipt. After the war he was named as the Chief of Police for Lake City from 1865 to 1870, so he did learn a new profession in the war.

Reuben Henry did have a life outside of martial conflicts. In the 1860 census Reuben Henry gave his profession as a merchant and valued his real estate assets at $1,500 and his personal assets at $7,000. The slave census records of that year show that he had seven slaves, one male (37), one female (39) and five boys between five and fourteen years, obviously the couple's children. In the 1870 census he lists his profession as a lawyer, but there are no records showing that he actually practiced law. By 1870 his assets had shrunk considerably to only $100 although his wife's real estate assets were $800 and her personal assets $400. Although his assets were small, it may be because he put nearly everything in his wife's name.

In her reminiscences of Civil War times, Lizzie Daughtrey reports that Mary Charles, Reuben Henry's wife, worked feverishly to prepare bandages and attend the wounded after the Battle of Olustee. After Reuben's death at the age of forty five, from what, we don't know, she worked as a music teacher. In fact, teaching music was her principal source of income since her husband had left her little to live on. On September 6, 1882, she married R. L. Markham but divorced him. She left some letters to her son Garret who, it appears, gave her a lot of worries. Her letters are very well written, no misspellings, even poetic at times; moreover she was proficient enough on the piano that she was able to teach that instrument, all of which indicates that she must have received a good education.

The death of her only child and son at the age of thirty three left Garret's wife, Callie, in poor financial circumstances, particularly since she had had three children under the age of six. Mary then took in and reared her only grandson, Rupert or Ruby, for ten years until she died on August 24, 1900, age sixty four. Reuben Henry and Mary are buried in Oak Lawn Cemetery in Lake City.

Child of Reuben Henry Charles and Mary Crews

Garret Vinzant, b. May 10, 1857; d. May 4, 1890; m. Tillithie Ann (Callie) Daughtrey on Oct 31, 1880.

Garret Vinzant Charles

Garret, or Garry, was born in Lake City, Florida, in 1857, on the eve of the Civil War. He was an only child, an unusual occurrence in those days, when most families, if they had children at all, could count their number on no fewer than the five fingers on the one hand. He attended some sort of school as is noted in the 1870 U.S. Census. On achieving adulthood he began working on the railroad, probably the Florida Southern, as an agent and telegraph operator. The 1885 Florida census shows that he was living with his young family in Orange County, Florida, and working as a railroad telegrapher. By 1890 he was living with his family in the small town of Reddick in Marion County, Florida, still working for a railroad, and it is there that he died later that same year.

Garry married Tillithie Ann Daughtrey in 1880. She was nicknamed "Callie," which was the name by which everyone knew her and, in fact, Callie is the name she gave on their marriage license. The Daughtrey family Bible gives her date of birth as 1856 although she said she was born in 1861 in the 1890 census. The earlier date is probably the correct one. After her husband's death she returned to Lake City, where she became a nurse midwife working for Dr. W. R. Chalker. There is no record of her having received any medical training, but she may have learned about a bit of medicine from her father, who, according to one source, had a lot of knowledge about herbal drugs. When her mother-in-law died in 1900, Callie moved into her home at 404 N. Alachua Street in Lake City, where she lived the rest of her life.

Very little is known about Garry since he died so young. He had no chance to make his mark in life except for the three children he left behind. In a letter his mother wrote him two years before his death she admonishes him not to take patent medicines, this advice indicating that he may have had a chronic illness. Apparently he had virtually no assets when he died causing his widow to take the drastic step of splitting up her family of three. She had just given birth to a little girl two months before he died. Moreover, she already had two other children; a boy of six and a girl of three. She kept her baby, Ethel, with her at home, and, as mentioned previously, she sent her son, Ruby, to live with his grandmother, Mary Charles. Her other daughter, Meta, went to live with her great aunt, Virginia Crews Harte, in Jacksonville.

Callie died of a stroke in 1929 at the age of seventy three. Her obituary in the Lake City newspaper stated that she was a little over seventy. It may be that she had fibbed somewhat about her age, since birth dates in family Bibles tend to be more accurate than census records. She was a member of the Advent Christian Church in Lake City, where her funeral services were held. Her good friend and relative, future Governor Fred Cone, was a pallbearer. Both Garry and Callie are buried in Oak Lawn Cemetery in Lake City. Their headstones give only their names, not their dates of birth and death.

Children of Garret Vinzant Charles and Tillithie Ann Daughtrey

1. Rupert Henry, b. Sep 1883; d. Jun 16, 1938; m. 1st Vivian Brown and 2nd Maude Isabelle Jenkins. Like his father he was a railroad man, having worked for the Atlantic Coast Line RR for thirty five years. His first wife died in 1920, and their two boys died shortly thereafter, apparently during the influenza epidemic. He remarried and had one son, R. H. Charles, who married but had no children. After his death in 1993 there are no living male descendants in this line with the surname Charles.

2. **Meta Aubrey, b. May 17, 1887; d. Sep 1, 1964; m. Lowndes Walton Shaw on Dec 15, 1909.**

3. Ethel Garry, b. Mar 28, 1890; d. Jan 25, 1947; m. William Karl Weaver. Weaver was a railroad man like his father-in-law and his brother-in-law, having worked at the Railroad Express Agency most of his life. Their son, W. K. or Buck, was a railroad executive with the Baltimore and Ohio Railroad, when he wasn't serving as an artillery battalion colonel in Europe during WWII.

Caroline Miller, Pulitzer Prize 1934

Caroline Pafford Miller was born on August 26, 1903 and died on July 12, 1992. She was the granddaughter of Rowan Pafford (1825-1890) who was the brother of Tillithie Pafford Daughtrey. That would make Caroline the second cousin of Meta Charles Shaw and therefore, our kinsman. Caroline published her Pulitzer Prize winning novel, *Lamb in His Bosom* in 1933 and the prize was awarded to her in 1934. Not only was it a prize winner but also a best seller and has been almost continuously in print since then. The Pulitzer Prize is awarded for a particular book, not for a body of work, as is the Nobel Prize. That is just as well for Caroline as she wrote only one more novel, *Lebanon*, which did not sell well and was generally panned. Today she is one of the least known of the Pulitzer winners, even in Georgia. Nevertheless, her relatives are very proud to be kin to her.

The Daughtrey Lineage

The first Daughtrey in this line is probably a James Daughtrey who was born about 1660, place unknown, and died about 1749 in

Isle of Wight County, Virginia. One of his sons was Thomas Daughtrey, born about 1693, perhaps in Nansemond County, Virginia, and died in Northampton County, North Carolina, in November 1757. He left a will that identified four sons: Samuel, John, Jesse and Thomas, Jr. This Jesse Daughtrey, born about 1735 and died in 1796 left a will that identified his sons: Lawrence, Henry, Thomas, Jesse, Starky and William, in that order. It is believed by most family researchers that this Thomas, son of Jesse, is our direct ancestor. In fact, Thomas sold a piece of land in December 1816 in Northampton County that he inherited from father, Jesse, and in the sales document he affirmed that by virtue of the will he had the right to sell the land owned by his father. This sale may have been just prior to his departure for Tennessee. I am not overly confident in this account since there were a lot of Daughtreys named Jesse, Thomas and Henry, but it is the best that I can provide.

An alternative take on Jesse being the father of Thomas, in this line, appears in a letter dated Sept. 9, 1936, written by Julien Soule, the daughter of Lizzie Daughtrey Soule, to her first cousin and our grandmother, Meta Charles. She writes a few words about the family's background, including the following, "Mother [Lizzie] says that John was Pa's grandfather and that his father was named Thomas and Thomas moved to South-east Tennessee when he had five sons and one daughter, Henry, William, Logan, Thomas J. and Arthur (grandfather Daughtrey) and Aunt Lizzie Daughtrey Green." If true then John, not Jesse, is Thomas's father. Go figure.

The information on Thomas Logan Daughtrey, below, should help illuminate all of this.

Thomas Daughtrey

Thomas Logan Daughtrey, the son of Jesse (or John) Daughtrey, was born about 1793 in Northampton County, North Carolina. Sometime between 1816 and 1818, he and his younger brother Henry moved to Tennessee, first settling in Williamson County, then sometime after 1825 but before 1830, he resettled near Harrison in Hamilton County, where he is found in that year's census. On March 4, 1816, he married Sylvia Smith in Northampton County, North Carolina, but, supposedly after her death, he married Elizabeth Gann in Hamilton County, Tennessee. It is believed that she was the daughter of Nathan Ignatious Gann and his wife Susan but no proof has been found. She was born about 1795. Both Thomas and Elizabeth died between 1860 and 1870 in Hamilton County

Children of Thomas Daughtrey and Sylvia Smith and Elizabeth Gann (not in order)

1. Henry, b. Mar 23, 1810 or 1814; d. Feb 26, 1895; m. Rhoda Curry about 1840.

2. Arthur, b. Jul 15, 1812; d. Oct 10, 1883; m. 1st Tillithie Ann Pafford in 1845 and 2nd Lenetta Carstarphen Bridges in 1865.

3. John A., b. 1815; d. 1892; m. Anna Alexander.

4. Edith, b. April 5, 1816; d. Jan 10, 1890 m. Calvin Corbitt.

5. Polly, m. a Mr. Green

6. Elizabeth or Lizzie, m. a Mr. Green.

7. Catherine, b. 1823; d. unk; m. Harrison "Dock" Frazier.

8.William Logan, b. 1832; d. unk. He served with the Union Army during the Civil War.

9. Thomas J., b. 1835; d. May 15, 1864; m. Cynthia Maddux. He enlisted in the Union Army, specifically Company "C" of the 5th Tennessee Volunteers, as a private, rising to the rank of captain. He was killed at the Battle of Resaca which is located between Chattanooga and Atlanta. After his death his widow married Hugh Francis Farris, a former Confederate soldier. Thomas's older brother Arthur served in the Florida militia with the Confederate forces. All the above is not only an example of the North/South sectional loyalties but, also, how they can be overcome.

Arthur Daughtrey

Arthur was born in North Carolina in 1812 the same year that saw the start of the second war with Great Britain. As a child he moved with his parents to Tennessee, where the family settled eventually on a farm in Hamilton County near the town of Soddy Daisy. Like the rest of his siblings he acquired some land and began farming. When he was in his mid-forties he decided to join a number of other family members who had resettled earlier in South Georgia. In about 1856 Arthur and his family packed up and moved by horse- and ox-drawn carts directly south from Tennessee to Columbia County, Florida, just below the Georgia state line. His brother, Henry, had settled in Clinch County, Georgia, which is on the Georgia line just above Columbia County, Florida. The earliest evidence of Arthur's arrival in Florida is February 1857 where the Land Office at Newmanville in Columbia County recorded his purchase of 110.16 acres of land in Section 24,

Township 35 located just to the northwest of present day Lake City on the north side of Jeffery Lake Road. There he built his home and became a fairly prosperous cotton farmer. Today most of this land remains used for farming and timber purposes although one up-scale subdivision, Spring Hollow, occupies a part of his former property.

Thanks to his daughter Lizzie, a little more is known of him than one might expect. In one account she wrote, "My father was the oldest of ten children and often had the responsibility of the family thrown upon his young shoulders. Therefore he lost the meager opportunity that the country offered at that time for an education. One year at school and what he learned at home was all he ever got. Yet he was a good scribe, a fine accountant and a good reader. Although he was never a politician, he took [an] active interest in all public matters, was full of patriotism, and always voted a Democratic ticket. In Tennessee he was an extensive grower. In Florida he tried to grow wheat and went so far as to have his machinery shipped to prepare it for market. When it was just beginning to mature, a rust [fungus] destroyed the entire crop. He then turned his attention to cotton which product at that time was "King Cotton" and was a most successful cotton grower".

While still in Tennessee, Arthur married Tillithie Ann Pafford, the daughter of James and Wealthy Corbitt Pafford. She was born in Cannon County, Tennessee, and was some sixteen years his junior and only fifteen or sixteen on her marriage day. One could speculate that he had been married previously because he was thirty three then, a relatively old age for a farmer's first marriage. But no such previous marriage has ever been found or even hinted at. Tillithie, also called Eliza, died in 1863 at the age of thirty five, leaving Arthur with six children between the ages of four and seventeen. On January 5, 1865, he married Lenetta Carstarphen Bridges, a widow with two children, who had relocated to North Florida to escape the fighting around Ringgold, her home in North Georgia. Arthur had rented a home to her and her in-laws on his plantation and, in this way, came to know her. He had seven more children with Lenetta who outlived him by almost thirty years, dying in 1912.

Arthur participated in two wars or conflicts. While still a young man in Tennessee he served as a sergeant in Benjamin Cannon's Company of the 1st Tennessee Mounted Infantry during the Cherokee War of 1836-37. His future father-in-law, James Pafford, and his mother-in-law's second husband, Isaac Curry, also served in that unit, while Arthur's brother Henry served in another volunteer unit at that time. The war is sometimes called the "Sabine War" and occasionally the "Cherokee Disturbance" but it was more like a police action. No fighting occurred and no soldiers were killed. In actuality the troop's role was to collect and force the Cherokees into stockades prior to their removal to Oklahoma territory.

When the Civil War broke out, Arthur was too old to serve in a regular unit. His daughter Lizzie claims that he was an advisor to Confederate General Joseph Finnegan at the Battle of Olustee, but there are no records to back up that claim. Nevertheless, as she also mentions, it is highly likely that Arthur did participate in organizing post-battle relief efforts and helping to bury the dead. Later he joined Capt. Roberts' Company of Florida Home Guards, serving from September 1864 until the end of the war. In 1907 his widow was granted a pension for services rendered in the war. See

Appendix C for Lizzie's account of the Daughtrey family during the Battle of Olustee.

In the 1860 Census he was living in Columbia County where he valued his real estate assets at $7,000 and his other assets at $4,000. Rather than having numerous slaves as his daughter, Lizzie, claims, the records show he had only two adult slaves. It is possible however that he purchased additional slaves before they were all freed five years later, or he rented slaves from other owners, because it was impossible to operate a large cotton plantation without a lot of labor, and slaves were about the only available source to fill those labor needs.

The Civil War and its aftermath would bring about a significant reduction in Arthur's prosperity. Some historians assert that Florida suffered more than most Southern states. The landed gentry—and Arthur might be included in this group if Lizzie is right—in central and west Florida found they had been greatly impoverished as agriculture shifted from a slave-driven cotton economy to a diversified farm and timber harvesting economy. Property values declined more steeply than even in Virginia, which had been devastated by war. Black Floridians were no longer enslaved but were still without property or means of support since cotton production fell. Some freed slaves stayed on with their former masters as is illustrated by one of Lizzie's stories. She tells about Dorcas, the house servant who looked after Eliza's children after the latter's death, and who had remained with the Daughtrey family until her own death many, many years after she had gained her freedom.

Florida had experienced little fighting during the war and, except for the Battle of Olustee, most skirmishes took place along the coast where war damages were relatively light. However, bands of deserters and "layouts" or draft dodgers had terrorized many civilians and caused some damage to farms and homes, but now, with the war over, it was expected that peace would bring about security. But this was not always the case. Lizzie tells about another incident in which some black Union soldiers on garrison duty in Lake City accosted their family home and threatened her father when he tried to protect his family. Shots were fired, livestock and fowl were killed and the children terrified. Although no one was hurt, it was only her father's courage and that of his wife that prevented the incident from getting out of hand. The Union captain of the soldiers later apologized to Arthur and then punished the offending soldiers, according to Lizzie, by hanging them by their thumbs for nine hours!

Without much cash from the sale of farm products, Arthur, like many others in the same circumstances, became more self-sufficient after the war's end. Gardens took on more importance, and the production of clothing at home compensated for a lack of money to purchase "store bought" clothes. In another area Arthur had a distinct advantage. Lizzie recalls that while still in Tennessee Arthur had learned about herbal medicine taken from plants such as Sampson snake root and Indian blood root, and tree bark from red and slippery oaks. She claimed that "Father never employed a physician in treating his family. He would select the healthiest cow in the lot, go to a doctor and get serum put in the cow. Then when she [the cow] broke out with the disease, he took the serum from her and vaccinated everybody on the plantation with his own little lance. We all carry the scars of that lance today. He preferred his own solutions for spring tonics from woods and barks and it was very seldom that a doctor was needed in our family. Never, except in acute cases or in confinement [was a doctor called] and even then he assisted and knew more than they did."

In the first census after the Civil War, that of 1870, the value of Arthur's real estate assets had declined to $2,000 and his personal assets to $1,500. Yet by the time of his death, his overall estate looked healthier. Since Arthur did not leave a will, the probate judge appointed his wife, Lenetta, and James Young, a Lake City merchant, civic leader and family friend as estate administrators. They determined that his wife, still with some seven dependent children at home, would receive a dower's portion of his estate valued at $785, mostly furniture and food stocks, to provide for her household. Lenetta was also deeded a 400 acre tract which included their home and farm buildings. This tract was only a part of his total land holding of 1,620 acres. The remainder of his non-real estate assets was sold at auction on December 20, 1884. Many of the items and goods were purchased by Lenetta and by his grown sons, Henry and Arthur (Jack) Daughtrey, and by his sons-in-law, Garret Charles and W. T. Hoover. The amount raised from this auction was $2,298.29 which was probably distributed among his children.

In June 1886 Lenetta petitioned the court to let her sell the remainder of his land, less the 400 acres she had inherited, to satisfy debts totaling $3,263, which the court granted. The land closest to Lake City, some 400 acres, was subdivided into 38 lots in size from 7.5 to 13.4 acres while the land further out consisting of 778 acres was subdivided into 19 lots in size from 3.8 to 80 acres. An auction was held on January 3, 1887, on the steps of the county courthouse where everything were sold. Lenetta, herself, purchased 32 of the 57 lots while W. R. Bush, an attorney and owner of the Lake City Water and Light Company, purchased eleven lots. Two of her sons and eleven other bidders purchased the remaining lots. The proceeds received from this auction were given to James Young to be used, in part, to pay off the debts.

Arthur is buried beside both of his wives in marked graves in Oak Lawn Cemetery in Lake City. Buried in the same plot are his son Henry and one of Lenetta's two daughters, Sarah, who never married. Other family members are buried in nearby plots, one of which happens to be the Charles family plot, where his daughter, Callie Charles, is buried with her husband.

Children of Arthur Daughtrey and Tillithie Ann Pafford and Lenetta Carstarphen Bridges (see note below)

1. Mary Magdalena, b. May 30, 1846; d. Jan 1, 1913; m. William Taylor Hoover.

2. Joseph Addison, Feb 8, 1849; d. May 14, 1922; m.1st Flora J. Bethea and 2nd Ada Reed.

3. Elizabeth Jane "Lizzie", b. Oct 23, 1852; d. Jun 8, 1941; m. E. J. Soule.

4. Arthur Wright, b. Jun 14, 1854; d. Feb 17, 1936; m. 1st Becky Hoover on Dec 4, 1881 and 2nd Fannie Daughtrey on Apr 24, 1929.

5. **Tillithie Ann "Callie," b. Sep 20, 1856; d. Apr 11, 1929; m. Garret Vinzant Charles on Oct 31, 1880.**

6. Henry Clay, b. Jun 19, 1859; d. 1895; m. Mary_____.

7. Thomas R.*, Oct 19, 1865; d. Aug 2, 1927; m. Anna B. Lancaster on Feb 8, 1891.

8. Martha Virginia*, Nov 6, 1867; d. May 16, 1929; m. A. R. Moore.

9. Magdalena*, b. May 4, 1869; d. Aug 14, 1951; m. Thomas D. Sealey, Dec 28, 1886.

10. Minnie A.*, b. Jul 18, 1871; d. Sep 28, 1958; m. W. R. Townsend

11. William Logan*, b. Oct 25, 1873; d. Jan 30, 1940; m. Bertha Sylvia Smith.

12. Oregon C.*, b. Jun 15, 1876; d. Nov 10, 1958; m. James P. Morgan.

13. Nettie*, b. Aug 20, 1879; d. Nov 12, 1883; never married

14. Mary E. Bridges**, b. 1857; d. Oct 2, 1935; m. H. J. Hodges.

15. Sarah J. J. Bridges**, b. Jun 24, 1858; d. Jun 24, 1918; never married.

Note: The first six children above were born to Arthur and his first wife, Tillithie; the second seven, marked with * to Arthur and his second wife, Lenetta. The last two children ** listed above were born to Lenetta and her late husband, Mr. Bridges, before she married Arthur.

The Crews Lineage

This Crews family originated, for our purposes, in the Colleton District of South Carolina. It is likely that our Micajah Crews was a brother of Alexander Crews in that the two of them jointly purchased a 1,000 acre tract of land there. If not brothers, then the two were very close relatives as well as being close in age. Alexander's father was said to be a John Crews, so that would be the name of Micajah's father, if the two were really brothers. However there is also a Joseph Crews in Colleton District who might be John's brother and Micajah's father, given that Micajah named his only son Joseph. Alexander and Micajah also came down to Georgia at about the same time and both settled in Camden County. Many of the Crews' family members moved on to North Florida, some to Duval County as in the case of Micajah's family, and others to Columbia County as in Alexander's case. A noted Crews descendant was Harry Crews, a prolific novelist from Bacon County, Georgia, who died in 2012, and who almost certainly is related to this Crews line although his exact lineage is unknown. Although best known as a novelist his best book is a semi-autobiographical account of growing up in the 1930/40's, the son of a poor sharecropper farmer in rural South Georgia.

Micajah Crews

Micajah, a delightful Biblical name that, alas, is seldom heard today, was probably born between 1765 and 1770, most likely in the Colleton District of South Carolina. We know that the name of his wife was Mary, and one researcher has claimed that her maiden name was Pugh, although no proof was given for arriving at this conclusion. Based on the birth of their first born they were married before 1795. He appears a number of times in Colleton County deed records, the first being when he purchased 906 acres of land on January 28, 1800, near the fork of the Big and the Little Saltketchie Rivers. He then acquired 342 acres on the Cow Pen branch of the Little Saltketchie River January 1, 1806, as well as 264 acres on the Big Saltketchie River, the records not indicating on which of the two rivers this acquisition took place. On August 25, 1809, jointly with Alexander Crews, he purchased a 1,000 acre tract on Black Creek off the Saltketchie's. All this land was in Colleton District of South Carolina. Micajah was enumerated in the 1800 U.S. Census as living in Colleton.

Sometime during the first decade Micajah decamped for Camden County, Georgia, where he appears in the 1820 census. It can be speculated that he left Colleton for Camden perhaps between 1811 and 1814 which is the same time that Alexander Crews is suspected of making the trek. The first county record of Micajah's presence there is when in 1819 he paid a total tax bill of $350 on "Pine Land" on the Great Satilla River, plus one poll tax and taxes on six slaves. He also appears in the 1820 Land Lottery in Camden. In the county inferior court records of 1821 Micajah was selected as a juror for the January term. In 1821 he acquired two-hundred acres on Port Road.

The fact that Micajah's last will and testament, dated Feb 9, 1823, was recorded in the Camden County Ordinary's Office, indicates that he died shortly thereafter, probably that same year. He divided his property among his wife, three living children, son-in-law and granddaughter; all were named in his will. He made his wife, Mary, and his "trustly" friend, Joseph Cone, the executors of his estate. His will is a very precise one, spelling out exactly who gets what and when. Mary survived him until, at least, 1830 when she is noted in the U.S. census for that year, still in Camden County. She does not appear in the 1840 census.

Children of Micajah Crews and Mary Pugh

1. **Joseph, b. 1794; d. 1850/60; m: Catherine Turner.**

2. Charity, b. 1796; d. 1857; m. John Starlings Goodbread in 1818.

3. Mary, b. unk; d. 1817; m. John J. North on Mar 8, 1816. Mary probably died in childbirth, leaving behind a daughter, Mary E. J. North. Her husband survived her by many years, dying in 1880 at the age of eighty eight. He married four times and had seventeen children, some by each wife. The oldest child, Mary above, was born in 1817 and the youngest in 1859, a difference of forty two years. Four of his sons, all by his second wife, died in the Civil War. He was a very prominent citizen of Clinch County, Georgia.

4. Esther A. B., b. Aug 22, 1803; d. 1893; m. William Haddock on Dec 22, 1830.

Joseph Crews

Virtually nothing is known about Joseph except the names of his children. He is found living in Duval County, Florida, in the 1850 Census with his wife Catherine Ann, forty five, and three children still at home but neither he nor his wife appears in the 1860 Census. His oldest child, Marie Ann, had married before the 1850 Census. His occupation was listed as farmer. He was fifty six in 1850, thus confirming his date of birth as 1794. He must have been a fairly prominent farmer in that his daughters married into well-known North Florida families, as will be seen below.

Children of Joseph Crews and Catherine Ann

1. Marie Ann, b. 1829; d. unk; m. William Smith on Nov 8, 1848.

2. Joseph C., b. Dec 4, 1831; d. Jun 21, 1899; m. Mary Catherine Lefils or Lefells. They are buried in the Old City Cemetery in Jacksonville.

3. Virginia "Jennie", b. 1835; d. Mar 20, 1911; m. 1st Oscar Harte and 2nd George Wells. Her first husband was the oldest son of Isaiah Harte, the founder of Jacksonville, Florida.

4. **Mary, b. 1836; d. Aug 24, 1900; m. Reuben Henry Charles in 1856.**

The Pafford Lineage

The first known ancestor in our Pafford line was a John Pafford, sometimes spelled in the early records as Parford, who died in 1786 in Surry County (later Stokes County), North Carolina. He was probably born about 1740. The name of his wife is unknown. We do not know where he was born or when he came to that county; however, deed records indicate that he appears in Surry County as early as 1778. He was the father of Thomas Pafford. From these same records we are able to name two other sons and a daughter but it is believed he had even more children.

Thomas Pafford

Thomas, the son of John Pafford, was born about 1764 in North Carolina, perhaps Rowan County, and died in June 1849 in DeKalb County, Tennessee. His wife Nancy was born about 1770 and died in the same county in May 1860. She may have been almost one-hundred years old, assuming the mortality schedules are correct. While there has been much speculation about the father of Thomas, deed records make it clear that Thomas was the son of John Pafford, above. One example is that on January 1803 Thomas sold one-hundred acres of land on a branch of Zelphy Island Creek adjoining Mitchell's line. This is the same one-hundred acre tract that was granted to John on November 3, 1784. And there are other such examples.

Deed and tax records indicate that Thomas and all of his family members left Stokes County about 1817 and by 1820 they are in Warren County, Tennessee, when they are recorded in the census taken there. A part of Warren County became Cannon County, while another part became DeKalb County; therefore the Paffords lived at one time or another in all three counties albeit in the same general area. As late as 1839 Thomas is buying and selling land in DeKalb County. It appears that he died at the age of about eighty seven, almost as long as his wife lived.

Children of Thomas Pafford and Nancy

1. William, b. 1796; d. 1878; m. Mourning Melton in 1818.

2. **James, b. March 19, 1797; d. Oct 1838; m. Wealthy Corbitt in 1823/4.**

3. John, b. Jun 24, 1798; d. Sep 15, 1851; m. Mary Sarah Melton in 1818.

4. Susannah, Aug 16, 1801; d. Sep 16, 1851; m. Thomas Lawrence in 1825.

5. Randolph, b. 1809; d. Oct 13, 1891; m. Mary Phillips in 1832.

6. Ethaney, b. 1812; d. unk.; m. Charles Hill in 1833.

Census records indicate there were two other daughters.

James Pafford

Universally called Jimmy, he moved with his family from North Carolina to Warren County, Tennessee. Around 1823/24 he married Wealthy Corbitt, the daughter of Isham and Amelia Stokes Corbitt, in Tennessee. They lived in DeKalb County, and in fact, the marker on his daughter Tillithie's headstone, states that she was born in that county, now Warren County. In 1834 he moved to Hamilton County, Tennessee, where he recorded a deed on Jan 19, 1835. It appeared that Hamilton County was his home place even though he died in Ware County in the part that became Clinch County, Georgia. According to family lore Jimmy came to that Georgia County with a drove of mules and horses to sell. He was taken ill and died in October 1838 at a place there that was later owned by the Lee family. His widow, Wealthy, soon afterwards relocated to that area, following several brothers, sisters and her mother, all of whom had preceded her to Georgia. After his death she married Isaac Curry and had several children by him. She died in 1860 in Clinch County.

Children of James Pafford and Wealthy Corbitt

1. Rowan, b. Apr 25, 1825; d. Jan 9, 1890; m. 1st Elizabeth Smith and 2nd Fannie Corbitt. He was the grandfather of Caroline Pafford Miller, and the father of sixteen children by two wives. He was a Georgia State Senator and Representative. He was also a

delegate to the 1861 Secession Convention for Coffee County and voted against secession. But he still served in the Confederate Army.

2. Tillithie Ann, b. Mar 10, 1828; d. Mar 20, 1863; m. Arthur Daughtrey in 1845.

3. Berrien, b. 1828; d. Oct 20, 1896; m. Hearty Sirmans in 1852.

4. James Marion, b. 1833; d. Sep 14, 1891; m. 1st Nancy Roberts in 1853 and 2nd Wealthy Corbitt, daughter of Newsom Corbitt, and not the same Wealthy that his father married.

The Harte Family of Jacksonville

The principal founder of Jacksonville, Florida, was Isaiah Harte, and the major bridge over the St. John's River downtown was named in his honor. Isaiah's two oldest sons were Ossian and Oscar, both lawyers. During the Civil War, Ossian was a Union sympathizer, and while he remained in rebel held Florida during the war, he generally kept his head down. After the war ended, he involved himself in politics, became the principal founder of the Republican Party in Florida, and in 1872 was elected Governor, but he died in office sixteen months later. Oscar never reached the heights of his brother, although he was well-known and, when the Civil War erupted, he joined the Confederate administration, eventually becoming a militia colonel. While Ossian remained married to one woman, Oscar married Virginia Crews, whom he later divorced. Now why is this so interesting to us, other than being a classic example of brother against brother? Virginia Crews is the sister of Mary Crews who married Reuben Henry Charles. Virginia is also the great aunt of Meta Charles Shaw, the three-year-old girl that Virginia reared in her home until she married nineteen years later. By the way, the divorce took place before Meta moved into Virginia's house.

Chapter 5

Our Parents
Theo and Meta

Descendants of Theo and Meta

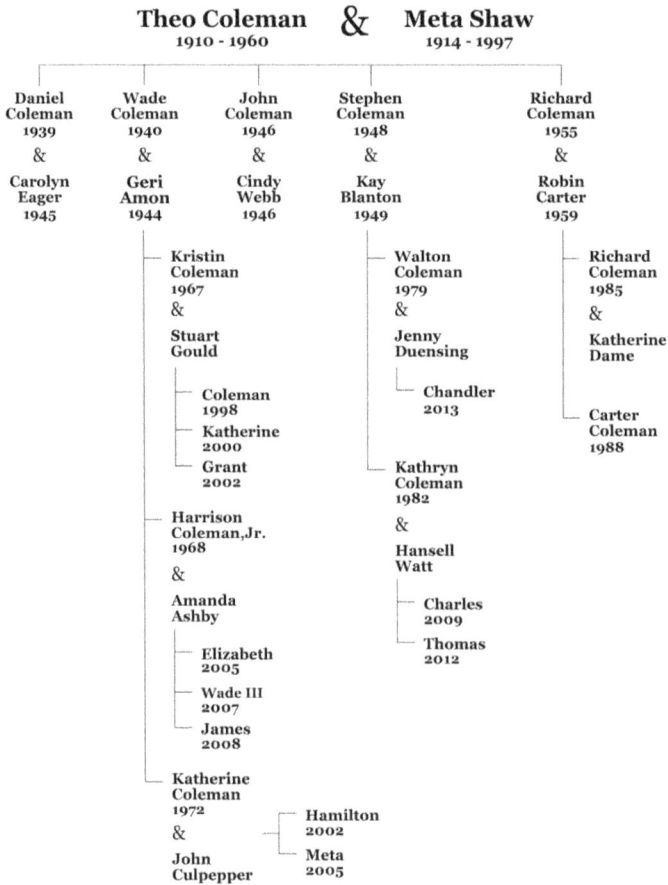

Theo Coleman & Meta Shaw
1910 - 1960   1914 - 1997

Daniel Coleman 1939	Wade Coleman 1940	John Coleman 1946	Stephen Coleman 1948	Richard Coleman 1955
&	&	&	&	&
Carolyn Eager 1945	Geri Amon 1944	Cindy Webb 1946	Kay Blanton 1949	Robin Carter 1959

Kristin Coleman 1967
&
Stuart Gould

- **Coleman** 1998
- **Katherine** 2000
- **Grant** 2002

Harrison Coleman, Jr. 1968
&
Amanda Ashby

- **Elizabeth** 2005
- **Wade III** 2007
- **James** 2008

Katherine Coleman 1972
&
John Culpepper

- **Hamilton** 2002
- **Meta** 2005

Walton Coleman 1979
&
Jenny Duensing

- **Chandler** 2013

Kathryn Coleman 1982
&
Hansell Watt

- **Charles** 2009
- **Thomas** 2012

Richard Coleman 1985
&
Katherine Dame

- **Carter Coleman** 1988

Note that the year below each name is the birth date.

Chapter 5

Our Parents
Theo and Meta

It is in this chapter that the four family trees come together to produce our complete family tree. Theo, our father, is the product of the Pine Barrens and the Between the Rivers lineages, that is, the Colemans and Hargroves, and their associated lineages. Meta, our mother, is the product of the Wiregrass Country and Florida Territory lineages, that is, the Shaws and the Charleses, and their associated lineages. Here is their story, the last one in our history.

Theo Wade, or just Theo, was born in 1910 in the small hamlet of Oak Park in Emanuel County, Georgia, which is on the Tattnall County line. His parents, Ernest and Alice, had moved there after a difficult year or so in Southern Alabama where his father had operated a turpentine camp. During his early years, when Theo's father was following various work opportunities, the family moved to several different towns in South Georgia before they settled down in Mineola, an unincorporated town just north of Valdosta in Lowndes County.

Theo attended various primary schools before enrolling in Valdosta High School. For his last year of high school he attended Georgia Military Academy in College Park, Georgia, a boarding school, graduating in 1929. His picture appears in the school's class annual, with some youthful comments: " 'Napoleon', First year G. M. A.; Commercial Course. Napoleon is seeking other schools to conquer. He hits Mercer University after his stay at the Academy. This man has a quiet, definite way which he expects to use in bar work—oh, yes, a lawyer, of course. Ah, Napoleon, would that thou couldst remain for the better acquaintance of a few years yet.'"

While he did not go to Mercer, he did study law by going directly to Cumberland University Law School in Lebanon, Tennessee, skipping undergraduate studies altogether. He graduated in 1931 after two years of study with a Bachelor of Laws degree. Nothing much is known about his higher education activities except that he was on the school's intramural baseball team and that he joined a fraternity, Lambda Chi Alpha, where he was an officer.

He was only twenty one when he graduated from law school. After passing the bar exam that same year and receiving his license to practice law on January 6, 1932, just three months shy of his twenty second birthday, he returned to Valdosta and, apparently, opened a law office. He also became active in community affairs by helping to found the Valdosta Junior Chamber of Commerce, becoming its first president. He joined the Elks Club and the Lions Club. In her autobiography, country music entertainer, Minnie Pearl, recalls her first professional engagement when she was still plain Miss Ophelia Colley. It was in 1934 and her agent had gotten her a job directing a local play in Valdosta: "I arrived in Valdosta for my first assignment. I was met by a Mr. Theo Coleman of the Lions Club. . .He was very nice and invited me to dine with him that night so that we could discuss preparations for the production. He had already lined up the cast and the chorus (I was to learn that this caliber of efficiency was the exception rather than the rule), and everything was ready for me to start rehearsals the next day. . .the play was a huge success. I left Valdosta thinking that the nicest people in the world lived there."

Theo became active in Democratic Party politics. In 1935, at the age of only twenty five, he was elected to serve the first of two terms representing Lowndes County in the Georgia State House of Representatives. Records show that he was an active member of the legislature despite his youth. During his time in office he sponsored a bill to allow the sale of alcoholic beverages only in state-owned package stores and he was in charge of a resolution to authorize a probe of Gov. Eugene Talmadge's administration.

He became a strong supporter of House Speaker E. D. Rivers and, later, when Rivers ran for Governor, Theo was his campaign manager in the 8th Congressional District. When the Legislature decided to honor a home-coming for President Roosevelt at Warm Springs, he was one of twelve members from both branches of the Legislature selected to work with Georgia's Congressional delegation in putting on the celebration. In a photo of this occasion he stands out as being the youngest member, by far, of the twelve legislators. Others in this photo include Marvin Griffin, a future Governor, and Roy Harris, a future House Speaker.

Theo seemed to be a young man in a hurry. An article in the *Valdosta Daily Times* contains extracts of the main address he made at a high school ceremony to honor the dead sponsored by United Daughters of the Confederacy. He even learned to fly a small airplane, in an age when most people had not flown, much less piloted a plane. In his reelection campaign in 1937, his opponent tried to capitalize on his penchant for flying by saying, with his eyes rolling skyward, that while everyone else was working and doing something productive, Coleman was way up there—just flying around, having a good time.

At a fish fry at the Twin Lakes Pavilion, probably sometime in 1937, Theo, the eligible bachelor, met Meta Aubrey Shaw, the second daughter of a prominent Valdosta family. Four years younger than Theo, Meta had been born and reared in Valdosta, although she had spent most of the years between the ages of five and twelve in Miami where her father was a real estate developer and builder, coming back to Valdosta only during the summers. Meta's childhood was a pleasant one. She took piano, art and dance lessons. One summer she went to Camp Chattooga in Rabun, Georgia, particularly for its dancing program, and another summer to Camp Cheonda at Lake Junaluska in North Carolina. She and her sister, Virginia, were constant companions; where one went the other one came along. Early on her father bought an automobile, at a time when few could afford that luxury. Her diary reveals a happy and well-adjusted child with many friends and loving parents.

After returning for good to Valdosta, she enrolled in the local public schools and graduated from Valdosta High School in 1931. Meta selected Florida State College for Women in Tallahassee, Florida, for her higher education, but, after her freshman year there, she transferred to the University of Georgia. She had pledged Phi Mu sorority at Florida State so she was accepted by that same sorority when she transferred to Georgia.

By all accounts Meta was a "big woman on campus." In her junior year she was elected to the presidency of the Phi Mu Chapter. A campus poll her senior year revealed that she was one of the four most popular students on campus. She was constantly being invited to and attending the most prestigious formal dances and events. Her major was journalism and she was initiated into the Theta Sigma Phi honorary journalism fraternity. She was the sponsor of an ROTC unit, a high honor is those days. Her avocation was dance, and she was a member of the University's dance club. For a while she wrote periodic articles, called News of the Campus, for the *Lowndes County Tribune*, in which she recounted events at the big state university.

There is a delightful photograph of Meta and Virginia, also a Phi Mu at Randolph Macon College, and two other sorority sisters, Sue Rollins, a life-long friend, and Janet Jarnagin, at a Phi Mu annual convention in Chicago. They posed in front of the Edgewater Beach Hotel where the convention was being held. They are arm-in-arm, dressed to the nines and are a stunning picture of health, youth and beauty. All four had driven themselves in L. W.'s Ford V8 from Valdosta to Chicago and back. Altogether

Meta would attend three Phi Mu conventions, and it was at those conventions that she probably made the contacts that would lead to her first job after graduation.

Meta graduated from Georgia on June 10, 1935 when she had just turned twenty one. Almost immediately she started her job as a Phi Mu national field director and moved to Evanston, Illinois, the sorority's national headquarters. Her main responsibility was to give advice and assistance to Phi Mu chapters, including appraising their performance. To do this she had to visit the various chapters under her bailiwick in the Midwest and Northeast mostly. Meta wrote many letters to her parents from the towns she visited as a part of her job. Her mother saved most of them, and, someday, they may end up in the possession of a Phi Mu chapter or its headquarters. During her three years at this job, she took some graduate courses at the University of Illinois but did not complete a degree.

In 1937 her father sent her on a European tour as a graduation present. She took a leave of absence from her job, and on June 19 she and a group of young women, mostly from the South, sailed from New York on the *M. V. Saturnia*. In her first postcard to home she wrote that "We are having a grand time. None of the officers or people on the boat speak good English so it is a perfect comedy trying to make them understand. The meals are grand—a million courses at each meal. We dock in Boston in the morning and will go on a sightseeing tour if we want to. I think I'll do it. Love, Meta." On the front of the postcard is a painting of the ocean liner on which they were travelling to Europe. The itinerary covered the British Isles, ten European countries, the Azores, Gibraltar and Algeria, all over a period of two months, including ocean crossings. Before she left she made an arrangement with the *Valdosta Daily Times* to write weekly travel stories that were printed in the newspaper.

When the tour was over she returned to Evanston until the end of spring term. She resigned to return to her parents' home in Valdosta to prepare for her wedding. Their formal dress wedding took place on November 11, 1938, at the First United Methodist Church in Valdosta. George Converse was best man while her sister, Virginia, was maid of honor. After spending their honeymoon in New Orleans they moved into a small apartment in the now razed Fry home, which was on the southwest corner of Patterson and Gordon Streets across from the Crescent. Meta became a housewife, and Theo decided not to run for reelection to the Georgia House. He also gave up piloting a plane but continued his law practice.

With the birth of their two oldest children, Dan in 1939 and Wade in 1940, they purchased a two-bedroom house at 305 E. Jane Street. Their home phone number was 790. When WWII began, Theo was thirty one years old, married and the father of two, with responsibility for managing the farm that Meta's father had given to her many years previously. Thus, he was in a low draft category. Nevertheless, as the military's manpower needs increased, especially in light of the upcoming Normandy invasion, Theo received his draft notice. His father was on the local draft board, but that made no difference. On March 25, 1944, just one week short of his thirty-fourth birthday, off he went to basic training at Ft. McClellan near Gadsden, Alabama.

While he was in basic training Theo hurt his back during a training exercise which put him in the hospital. The story is that he had lost so much weight that his uniform became very baggy. Once when he had to flop to the ground, a can of rations he was carrying on his body dislodged itself and he fell on his back on top of it. Apparently he chipped a vertebra that would bother him the rest of his life.

Yet the accident was a blessing in one important way. The soldiers in his training unit were all part of the European invasion force a few months later and many of them did not return. With his legal training and background, he was transferred to a military intelligence unit where he spent the rest of the war tracking down deserters and draft dodgers. Part of the time he was stationed at Camp Sibert, Alabama, but by the end of the war he was working out of Atlanta. His outfit was the 1428th Special Command Unit, District 4, and it might have been involved in a variety of intelligence activities. It appears the unit was disbanded after the war, and I have never been able to find any information about it. Could he have been sent to Cuba?

There are three intriguing photographs of him in his uniform in Havana, Cuba, probably in 1945. One photo consists of a large group of men in American and Cuban uniforms, and some men and women in civilian clothes on the deck of a ship. Theo, in his uniform, is kneeling on the front row. Two other photos were taken in Sloppy Joe's Bar, one with him, still in uniform, and a Cuban man in a suit while the other is of Theo as well, the same man, another soldier and a well-dressed woman. To this day we do not know why he was in Cuba and who all those people are.

With Theo away in the Army, Meta's financial situation became difficult in that she was trying to live and raise her family on a private's pay. Having a garden and raising chickens in the back yard helped only a little. To gain a little more income, Meta rented out one of their bedrooms to an airman in training at Moody Air Force Base and his wife. She and her two sons then shared the other bedroom. Finally Meta decided to rent the entire house to two Air Force couples, and all three moved into Grandmother Shaw's big house on Ashley Street, only two blocks away.

On August 31, 1945, Theo was honorably discharged from the Army and returned to Valdosta to be reunited with his family and to resume his law practice. He also continued his interest in politics, becoming a member of the county Democratic Party committee and, later, its chairman. Only three months after he left the Army, Gov. Ellis Arnold appointed him to a four-year term as the Valdosta City Solicitor and, although this was only part-time, it supplemented his private law practice. In 1947 Gov. Thompson, in his role as the Commander of the Georgia National Guard, appointed him to the rank of Lieutenant Colonel and Aide de Camp on the Governor's staff, really an honorary position but nice.

In 1946 they had a third child, John, and it was clear that the house on Jane Street was becoming too small, so, with another pregnancy—that would be Stephen—on the way, they decided to build a new and larger house. After selling the Jane Street home, they moved into a small house on Marion Street while the new one at 114 High Street was being built. In 1948 they moved into that house which would remain the family home for next sixteen years. Meta also decided to open a nursery school, first in her home, and, later, as it became more successful, she moved the school to a building she constructed in the back yard. This business provided an income boost for the growing family while, at the same time, it permitted her to follow the local school schedule and close it down for the summer.

Most of those years, Meta had a full-time maid, a black woman named Cora Cornelius, who also looked after her children and helped with the nursery school. Meta said she could never have survived all those years without Cora's help, and, even though Cora left her employ when she closed the school and moved to the country, they stayed in touch. As Cora's health declined Meta would go by her apartment at the Ora Lee West homes and bring her little gifts and some fast food, and the two of them would sit and chat for a long time about those days on High Street.

In 1955 their fifth and last son, Richard, was born. Life on High Street was nothing less than tumultuous. The five boys were involved in all kinds of activities, including Cub and Boy Scouts. The neighborhood was full of children of all ages and impromptu games and sports were common entertainment. They belonged to the Valdosta Country Club, so a lot of time was spent there in the summer with the boys swimming and participating in other sports. Membership in the First Methodist Church was important, with Sunday school and services, Wednesday night supper, youth fellowship and revivals to go to. Appendix "D" is her account of the good life on High Street.

As the years passed, Theo's role in family life declined. He had never regained the vigor he had before the war, and his dependence on alcohol increased. During the last years of his life his law practice was almost at a standstill; and he was spending more and more time at the farm where he stayed frequently in an old vacant house on the property. In February 1961 he took his own life.

His death was a shame because it was the end of a fine lawyer and talented man. He was well-read, smart, with lots of charm and undoubtedly distinguished. At six feet in height, with straight black hair, he was impressive looking, particularly when he dressed in a dark, double breasted suit, his favorite business attire. He was articulate and performed well in a court room. Many of his friends and colleagues had thought he would be Georgia's governor one day.

Once, in the mid-fifties, a horrific crime took place in Lowndes County in which a county Deputy Sherriff, Dick Waldron, was gunned down capriciously after he stopped a drifter's car for a traffic violation. Theo was retained to assist the County Attorney, who had little trial experience. Courtroom seats at this trial were at a premium, but some of us were able to attend. I still remember Theo's voice and look when he pointed at the murderer and, with eyes flashing and chin jutting forward, Theo called him a "mad dog killer." He was convicted and sentenced to death, but the sentence was overturned because of a mistake the County Attorney made.

There was an incident in which Theo did both himself and his family proud. Their farm was located just south of Moody Air Force Base and often the overhead jets could be seen and heard easily. One day in June 1956 a pilot crashed nearby in his jet, and Theo and another man responded. Col. Robert Worden, the Moody base commander, put it best in a letter to the *Valdosta Daily Times*: ". . .two of your neighbors risked their lives in rescuing an Air Force Officer. Although in imminent danger of bodily harm from the burning aircraft during the entire rescue, Mr. Raiford Sapp and Mr. Theo Coleman unhesitatingly evacuated

Lt. Stanley Hooks from a crashed F-89D seven miles from Moody and rushed him to a hospital."

The pilot's father, D. L. Hooks, wrote from his heart to Theo when he declared that, "Had it not been for your great kindness and resourcefulness in my son's hour of need, he would not be alive today. . .I thank you with all my heart, for had he died there in the swamp, the grief that my wife and I would have borne, would have been overwhelming." There are few of us who have the opportunity to save another person's life; Theo did.

After his death Meta was left alone with five sons between the ages of six and twenty one, two of whom were in college while the youngest had just started school and all would eventually go to college. To meet those expenses she decided to earn a teaching degree and she did so by attending night school at Florida State University, receiving a Master of Science Degree in Pre-School Child Development. To achieve her goal she had to drive several times weekly to Tallahassee at night, often with her youngest son, Richard, in the car. After graduating and receiving her teaching certificate, she closed down her nursery school and began a career with the Valdosta school system.

Her graduation took place on April 18, 1964, and it was a proud and happy day for her and for her sons. In fact, her sons were so proud that they, with immense help from a few of her best friends, held a surprise graduation party for her at the county club. It was also her fiftieth birthday and well over one hundred friends and family members showed up. Until her death she swore that she did not have the slightest inkling of the surprise event, which, by the way, she enjoyed immensely and often talked about it.

Another important decision was to lease the portion of the farm used for agriculture for a steadier source of income, while still leaving her the forest lands on which she could harvest timber. She also decided to sell her home on High Street and to build a new house on her farm land on Knight's Academy Road. In mid-1964 the High Street house was sold and the new one occupied. Many people felt that her new home was way too far out of town. Even the two roads to it were not paved, and it was many years until they were. It was a large home with five bedrooms and three and one-half baths. It had plenty of room for her sons and their growing families when they came over. She loved living in the woods, she said. She always stated that her main interests in life outside of her sons involved wildlife and plants. The quiet and solitude of country life also suited her.

Her career as a school teacher lasted some fifteen years. She started teaching first at the Southeast Elementary School, and it is believed that she was the first white teacher in that virtually all-black student body. She then transferred to the Pine Grove Elementary School where she taught in the same grade. In 1967 she helped start the Head Start program in the Valdosta school system and served as its first director until 1972. After leaving that job, she taught for five years at the private Valwood School and headed up the lower school division. After retiring from teaching at the elementary school level, she taught night classes in child care at Valtech, now Wiregrass Tech, which were aimed at students who aspired for a career as kindergarten and Head Start teachers.

Her involvement in her community was legendary. She was an active member of the American Association of University Women, and served a term as chairman of the Valdosta chapter. She was also one of the founders and the first president of the South Georgia Association of Young Children. She was a charter board member of the Food Bank, now Second Harvest of South Georgia, and with Bill Eager, Jr., she served on the committee to identify and hire its first full-time manager, Frank Richards, who is still in that position. She served as a member on the Mental Health Board. She participated in the Literacy Volunteers of America program and for many years tutored both youth and adults to read.

One of Meta's lifelong interests was expressed through her membership in Valdosta's First United Methodist Church, where she was baptized and married. She taught Sunday school there for many years and served on the Christians Concerns Commission and the Administrative Board. She also made sure her sons attended services and other church functions.

After retiring, Meta renewed her interest in traveling, something that had eluded her since her marriage. But what else could one expect of someone who had worked constantly and reared five sons over almost four decades. Many of these trips were in the company of her sister, Virginia, also a widow, or her youngest son, Richard. Most were in the U. S. or to nearby countries: Alaska, Hawaii, the western U. S. and New England, but also the Caribbean/Panama Canal and Canada. One exception was a visit to the African country of Zaire or Congo—the name changes frequently—where her son, Dan, was living and working in Kinshasa, the capital. After visiting him she traveled on to Kenya to visit some game parks. She brought back many souvenirs and wonderful memories that she loved sharing with others on her return.

One of her accomplishments was discovering that she had Revolutionary War soldiers in her background. As mentioned in a previous chapter her mother's efforts in this matter had been in vain and she and her sister were sorely disappointed. Meta located not one but two ancestors who played a role in that war, the husband and wife team of Thomas and Elizabeth Horne. While Thomas fought, Elizabeth, after his death, sold provisions to the Continental Army. This qualified Meta for DAR membership under Elizabeth, and she took advantage of this opportunity.

For many years Meta had suffered from arthritis and bronchiectasis, a lung disease that got progressively worse as she aged. In 1986 she felt chest pains, and after being diagnosed with blocked arteries, she underwent heart bypass surgery. Meta's ailments worried her sons, insofar as she was still living alone in her country home, so, after much discussion, she agreed to relocate to Valdosta. In 1989 she sold her home, along with forty adjoining acres, which still left her with about five-hundred acres, and built a new house at 3204 Ridgefield Lane. Now that she was closer to her sons' homes, she was able to spend more time with her grandchildren. She even fixed up a room with toys and games for them to play with when they visited. There seemed always to be an on-going jigsaw puzzle on the card table.

Meta's last six or seven years were difficult for her. She was often in pain and too often miserable. Her lungs deteriorated to the point that she had to use an oxygen tank which limited her mobility. She wondered why the doctors were unable to cure her, and she kept seeing different specialists in the hope that one would be able to do so. But the lung disease was incurable. She refused to go into a nursing home and instead relied on home health care workers. She made a number of overnight stays in the hospital. But she was a fighter and wanted to live. Finally she made one last trip to the hospital where she died on October 20, 1997.

After Theo's death she had purchased a double lot in Sunset Hill Cemetery in Valdosta for his burial. Three days after her death she was laid to rest beside him, more than thirty seven years later. She was eighty three years old.

Children of Theo Wade Coleman and Meta Aubrey Shaw, all of whom were born in Valdosta and are still living there:

1. Daniel Shaw (Dan) b. Oct 2, 1939; m. Carolyn Hall Eager on Nov. 27, 2009. Dan graduated from the University of Georgia, served a three-year hitch in the U. S. Army, mostly in France with the 249th Engineer Battalion, and then spent two years in Venezuela as a Peace Corps Volunteer. He is an Eagle Scout. Dan had a career in international development, working for a number of consulting firms involved in foreign aid programs. He lived and worked in Colombia, Barbados, Congo, Ireland and Poland, in addition to carrying out assignments in over forty countries worldwide, all while being based in the Washington, D. C. area. He moved back to Valdosta in 2002, where, after a lifetime as a bachelor, he married Carolyn. In retirement he has been active in a number of volunteer activities such as serving as a member of the Valdosta Symphony Orchestra Board including a term as its chairman, as well as a board member and chairman of The

Salvation Army in Valdosta. For several years Dan volunteered with Habitat for Humanity which included leading a team of volunteers to build houses in Argentina. He collects first editions by and about Georgia writer Flannery O'Connor when he is not plugging away as the family historian and genealogist. He attends the First United Methodist Church.

Paffords of Texas and Georgia

Once upon a time there were two Pafford brothers in Tennessee. John (1798-1851) went to Texas where his son, Thomas, married a young lady named Delana Hall whose brother was Calvin Hall. Calvin was the second great grandfather of a girl named Carolyn Hall who moved in 1970 to Valdosta, Georgia. The other brother, James (1797-1838), settled in Georgia and was the third great grandfather of a boy named Dan Coleman who moved back to Valdosta in 2002 where he had been reared. Then one day Dan and Carolyn married. Moral of the story: Watch whom you marry. You could be related, in this case, by marriage, not by blood. But it was a close call.

---

2. Wade Harrison, b. Sep 30, 1940; m. Geri Amon on Oct 2, 1965. Wade graduated from Vanderbilt University with a Bachelor's degree and then received his law degree in 1965 from the University of Georgia. He is the senior partner of the Coleman Talley Law Firm with offices in Valdosta and Atlanta. Wade is a member of the American, Georgia and Valdosta Bar Associations. Other professional memberships include the American College of Trial Lawyers; the Southern Judicial Circuit Bar Association; Georgia Defense Lawyers Association; and International

Association of Defense Lawyers. Wade was a supporter of his fellow Georgian, Gov. Jimmy Carter, who appointed him to the Georgia Board of Natural Resources, where he served a term as Chairman. When Carter ascended to the Presidency, Wade and Geri visited the Carters at the White House, spending three nights in the Lincoln Bedroom. Wade is an Eagle Scout. He was a member and president of the Valdosta Symphony Orchestra Board as well as a Board member and former chairman of First Federal Savings and Loan. Wade is General Council and a permanent member of the Board of Trustees of the Valdosta State University Foundation and a former member of the board of the Georgia Historical Society. Wade has served as a director and president of the Valdosta Boys and Girls Club, the Valdosta County Club and the Valdosta-Lowndes County Chamber of Commerce. He has served as Senior Warden of Christ Episcopal Church. He and Geri have three children, Kristin, Harrison and Katherine, and eight grandchildren.

3. John Walton, b. Jul 28, 1946; m. Cynthia Webb in 1971. John graduated from the University of Georgia with a Bachelor's degree. He moved to Jacksonville, Florida, where he joined Atlantic National Bank. After leaving the bank, he was employed as a commercial real estate broker with Rogers and Taylor in Jacksonville. He relocated to Valdosta in the early 1990s where he continued to work in the area of commercial real estate with several different firms. He is divorced from Cindy and is now retired.

4. Stephen Charles, b. Feb 8, 1948; m. Kay Blanton on Nov 24, 1973. Steve graduated from Valdosta State University with a Bachelor's degree in accounting; he is also a member of Kappa

Alpha Fraternity. After graduation he served a three-year hitch in the U. S. Army as an explosive ordinance disposal specialist. Initially he joined the Citizens and Southern National Bank in Valdosta, but left after a few years to supervise the operation of Blanton Farms which he still manages. He began a career in real estate, eventually opening his own firm in 1983, Coleman Realty. Eight years later he joined two other realtor brokers to open a branch of REMAX, which he managed until 2011 when the company was sold. He continues to work today at a slower pace as a real estate salesman. He has served for over twenty years on the board of The Salvation Army, and is a former board member of the Valdosta Historical Society. Steve attends the First United Methodist Church, where he has served on the Board of Trustees and the staff parish committee. He and Kay have two children, Walton and Kathryn and, so far, three grandsons.

5. Richard Lowndes, b. Jan 14, 1955; m. Robin Carter on Dec 19, 1981. Richard graduated with a Bachelor's degree from the University of Georgia, an MBA from Valdosta State University and a law degree from Mercer University. He joined the Coleman Talley Law Firm in 1985 where he is a partner. He is a member of the Valdosta Bar Association, the American Bar Association, the State Bars of Georgia and Florida. Richard is the consummate outdoorsman and loves nothing better than to be out on his farm—all of which is an original part of our Grandfather Shaw's farm—to hunt and roam the woods with his dog. Richard is a member of Christ Episcopal Church where he has served as warden. He and Robin have two sons, Rick and Carter.

Appendices

Appendix A

Thomas Horne's Revolutionary War Letters

Dare and Loving wife and family—These fue lines come to let you know that I am very unwell and grately uneasy about you all. Hoping these lines will find you and all of our family well, and with all to let you know that we have had a Battle 28 of June which lasted for 7 ours tho with good success on our side. We lost but ten men killed and som cripple. I do expec to have a grate many more battles yet for there lies about 45 sale of men of war which we do expeck to fier on us every Day. Pray my Dare Wife do not be uneasy about me nor none of the Family tho I suffer Grately. I shall hier a man in my Room as Soon as I can tho they do ask a great deal of money. I have sent you a hundred pounds for yoor use and Family as yoo think fit to use it. Pray my Dare Creetur be as well satisfied as yoo can until I com. And I remember my love to Saley and Dickey and all the Rest of the Family and to yoo my Dare Wife from yoor loving Husband till Death.

THOS. HORNE.

June ye 29 Day 1776

John Hood Desires to be remembered to yoo all and his Family.

To Elisabeth Horne these Living on flat Creek near Mr. Jacksons pr faver of John Jones.

—o—

Dare and Loving Wife and Family. These fue lines com to let you know my sad Confinement and Hardships. We are all most naked for want of Clothes and sufer nearly for provishons and in no wise Likely to be any better of for the vessel lies their still. My Dare Wife I recd yoor Letter Rote by Roe and it informed me that yoo was likely to sufer as yoo had not got all the money I sent yoo. But I hope yoo have got the hole money by Roland at last. Pray my Dare Wife Bare these mis fortunes of our being apart So long with as mutch pashance as yoo can until I com to yyoo agen which I hope will not be long with God's assistance I do entend to hier a man in my room and Com Home to yoo. So no more my Dare wife and family But I remain yoor Loving Husband until Death.

THOS. HORNE

N.B. remember me to Saley and Dicky, pore Creters.

Sullivan Island July ye 26—1776. To my Dare wife Elisabeth Horne.

To Mrs. Elisabeth Horne these flat Creek pr faver of Mr. Welch.

—o—

Dare and Loving wife these fue Lines coms to let you know that I am in good helth at present, Thanks be to God for it. Hoping these fue lines will find you the same and all our family Likewise and With all to Enform you that I Hant Receved any Money Sence I was at Home But Do Expect to git paid the Last of this month and then to Com Home for Sum time So my Dare wife make out as well as you Can until I Com Home which I hope will be By the time I above said tell John Riles that I have sold His Horse for twenty pounds Ruf as He Runs and will pay him the money when I com Home and Do expect to git that money of Proctor But Han't yet the pot and pan is quite Lost So he Nede not troble Himselfe any more for the money He Shall Have. My Dare wife Remember me to Francis Griffin and His wife and tell Him to List a man for me as Soon as He can if He pleses for I am Bent to git Clare of the Ridgment By June at furderst & tell Him Furder that Bateman Depends on Him as soon as possible He will Send or Bring Him a man tell Him pray Don't fale giting me a man and I will Have the money Ready to pay Him. Pray my Dare Wife Send me a fue Lines by the first chance to Let me know How you are in Helth and other ways in So Nomore at present But I Remain your Dare and Loving Husband until Death. Remember me to Dickey and Saley.

March ye 22 Day 1778   THOS. HORNE

—o—

September ye 22 Day 1778

Dare and Loving wife and family these fue Lines Coms to Let you know that I am in a very pore State of Helth at present But Sum whate mending But very weke and pore So as I am not able to

Com Home once more tho I am all moste Crasey to Com to See you all once more and Can not at present tho I hope it will not be very Long Before I Cum with Gods Help So my Dare wife I Hope these Lines will find you and our famly all in good Helth and Mr Griffin and His wife and family all so and with all to Enforme you my Dare wife that my Long spell of Sickness with my Long Gurney to East Flarida Has taken all my wagers So that I Cant be able to Help you at present which I am in Grate fare you are in Grate want I Have about one Hundred and forth pounds Due to Me which I Hope to git before Long and then to Come Home if posable I Can my Dare wife tell Mr Griffen to git a man in my Room and I will gave Him one Hundred pounds and if He can to Bring Him Down to town as soon as posable for I am not able to Stay in the Ridgment any Longer   Remember me to Delyah and her Baby and Saley and Dickey and them all for I Love to see you and them all my Dare— So I have nomore to Rite to you my Dare wife at present   But remain your Loving Husband.

THOS. HORNE

—o—

September ye 10 Day 1778

    Dare and Loving wife and Children and all frends these fue Lines Come to Let you all know that I am in a very Loe State of Helth Still, But Sum what mended not able to Com Home But Live in Hopes to Com Soon and Do want if posable for Mr Griffin to Enlist a man in my Room with out Fale and Contrive Him Down to town and am at Grate expense   Every Day to git any thing as I can Eate which I Cant eate any of what is allowed me as I am so Sick

So my Dare wife and Children I Hope to be with you Before Long if God is willing So pray Desier Mr Griffin to try if he pleses to Git a man very Soon and Send Him Down and I will pay Him well for His Troble   my Dare wife I Have sent you five leters and never Hae Had one from you which I think very Hard of so I Hope these Lines will find you and the Children and Mr Griffins and His family all in good Helth—So I Have no more to Rite to You my Dare wife at present But remain Your Loving Husband till Death.

THOS. HORNE

Appendix B

The Reuben Charles Papers, 1816-1832 from the Virginia Shaw Girardin and Meta Shaw Coleman Collection

This collection contains correspondence, bills of sale, merchandise lists and other information documenting the management of Moses E. Levy's Pilgrimage Plantation in Alachua County between 1824 and 1826. Reuben Charles acted as Levy's manager. Letters refer to planting and construction at the plantation. See also the David Levy Yulee Papers, held by the library.

Donated April 3, 1998, by Daniel S. Coleman, Wade H. Coleman, and David L. Girardin in memory of Virginia Shaw Girardin and Meta Shaw Coleman.

Davis Floyd to Reuben Charles concerning house construction, 8/17/1824

Text of the first page:

St. Augustine 17th Augt. 1824

Dear Sir

Since the departure of Mr. Levy I have received a letter from Mr. Edwards the person who is engaged in building a house for Mr. Levy—it would seem from that letter that there is some misunderstanding on the subject and as Mr. Levy has not informed me the state of the case I am at a loss what to say. This much I would suggest, that it is probable that Mr. Levy did intend with the team to furnish a driver and I would recommend, first that in no event should the crop be neglected, but should there be leisure times when the hands will be doing but little to have the Halling done, and not let the work stop on that account. If Mr. Levy did promise Mr. Edwards to furnish a driver as well as a team and should have made no arrangement with you to do so, you are too well acquainted with his character for justice & honesty to imagine for a moment that he would hesitate for a minute to make you an adequate remuneration.

Mr. Levy has written you that—

Davis Floyd to Reuben Charles, 9/1/1825

Text of the letter:

Mr. R. Charles

Sir Young Mr. Levy having determined to return to the plantation to stay, you will please provide for him in the manner pointed out by his father, and also let him have a horse for his own use. I think if you can spare the waggon and team that you had better send soon for the wheat and oats to sow. I would also advise that five or six bushels of the wheat should be sowed about the middle of October, the best way to sow is to flush up the ground well and sow on the grain and afterward harrow it in and if the land is stumpy to send a hand or two with hoes to chop around the stumps and have all the sprouts well cut off--I would also advise that one or two bushels of the wheat be retained to sow about the last of February, and all the oats to be sowed about that time, when the hands come down with a boat to Six Mile Creek. I must have notice so that I may send out cart and horse to the landing. I have given Col. Humphreys your note which I hope you will take up.

I am respectfully, e& e&

David Floyd

1st Sep. 1825

Appendix C

Lizzie Daughtrey's Civil War Story

My father's time in the Civil War was mostly employed in looking after the sick and the families of those who were in the army. He was not called to the ranks because of white swelling in one leg, but was a home guard and served in that capacity until the end of the war. He had an honorable discharge and my stepmother drew a pension up to the time of her death. I always thought father one of the greatest characters I ever knew in fact he had more executive ability than most men. He could set more people to work at different tasks and saw that each fulfilled his task to the letter, and [he] did it with seemingly no effort. A word of command from him was sufficient. His keen sense of honor was his safeguard at all times. His word was his bond, his honor was his life.

During the war he did many noble things which should have been recorded. One morning he arose early, saddled his big Kentucky mare, ate a hurried breakfast, and was soon out of sight. Of course, none of us dared to question [him] but we knew there must be something unusual going to happen. When he arrived at Lake City he found General Finegan on the shores of Lake Isabelle, the men throwing up embankments to hide behind for battle. In his blunt way, he said, "My God, Finegan, are you going to have the fight right in the midst of the women and children?" To this

Finegan replied, "What else can I do, Mr. Daughtrey? Here is the telegram which read, 'They are going to eat dinner in Lake City today.'" Then, Father told him he would lead if he would follow and they would meet Mr. Yankee at Ocean Pond. That is just why and how the battle was fought at Olustee. Mr. Finegan had known father for years, was one of his cotton buyers and was willing to be guided by his better judgment.

It was very late that night when he returned home. We children, Jack, Callie, Henry and myself were all asleep in his bed and he lay down on a cot in the same room but not to sleep. When I awoke next morning he was standing in the front door. I heard a rumbling like distant thunder and asked if it was thunder or if it was a storm. No, said he, "it's a battle just twelve miles away but don't be afraid". But, as you know, I certainly was afraid and ran in the kitchen and to Mama Dorcas. She said she had heard it and knew the Lincoln soldiers were coming to set her free. I then went back to the front door and Newton Handack was at the gate. He called me to him and said, "Go tell your father to come here quickly and bring me something to eat". I told father, then told Mamma and she gave me some cold baked potatoes and boiled ham, and I took it to him. He ate that cold stuff, and meanwhile told us how he had ridden through the woods and swam creeks to tell the news of the battle as the routes had all been cut. There was no other means of spreading the news.

By three o'clock that afternoon several trains had arrived bringing the dead and wounded from the battlefield. Father had two teams at work hauling the wounded to the Carthey home, the Hancock house, A. J. T. Wright's store and to every church in Lake City. The doors had been thrown open for their use. The Grey and the Blue fared alike for the nurses and doctors all acted on the one principal of a common sympathy for all. Every one there was some mother's son. Among those taking part in caring for those soldiers were Mrs. Mary Charles; Misses Frankie, Mary, Martha and Dora Hancock; Mrs. Carthey; Mrs. Baxley; and many others. Mother McNeil gave her two feather beds to make pillows for their heads. The dead were hauled to the cemetery where my father had ordered trenches fixed, except those whose names or address were pinned to them. These had separate graves, but on account of the situation and the general rush they were buried four deep in the trenches. Four days and nights we saw nothing of father, except just home for a few minutes to get the eggs and jelly jams, milk, hams and everything our little hands could get together for the nourishment of those sufferers, and at last when the wagons were brought home, we could not go near them for the terrible odor. One peculiar thing about it was that Jack one of our faithful old mules who lived to gain his freedom and lived long after that, would never again allow himself to be harnessed to either of those teams. He seemed to have a horror of them [and] no matter what we did to fix them, it made no difference to him for he was forever done with them.

Now, you will wonder why my big sister did not share in all these trials and tribulations. She had gone over to Suwannee County with Brother Joe with the slaves of several families of Jacksonville and Lake City. When the rumor reached Jacksonville that the Federal Army was approaching, Drs. Daniels and Leangle, Judge Baker and some others sent their slaves up to Lake City requesting father to take care of them. He did not only theirs, but those of Colonel Wright and his son, except old Mamma and

Steven, which were all that were left. Just think of a girl seventeen and a boy of nineteen [actually he was fifteen] taking charge of more than two hundred slaves and piloting them to a place of safety. It was a most hazardous undertaking but they were well armed and knew no fear. Only one of them escaped, a young man belonging to my father whose name was King, [who] took a gun from Joe's buggy and hid in a thicket. They decided not to pursue [him] as that might cause more trouble. King reached the Federal lines and got mustered into the battle, broke ranks, disobeyed orders and was sent to Dry Tortugas [federal prison] where he soon pined away and died.

Another thing that I like to recall is that during the war a federal captain was put in jail at Lake City, suspected of being a spy. My father visited the jail and heard his story. He had been appointed to the charge of a Negro company and not having had any experience with the colored race, he failed to be able to control them. By some means, Mr. L. N. Johnson and my father managed to get him out of prison and two years he made his home at their home. His only means of recompense was to take his uniform, go to Cedar Keys, don his blue suit and run the blockade at Bocagrande. He would give the salute to those grim monsters of the sea called gunboats, pass between them, go to Savannah and return with dry goods, coffee, tea and many other articles that it was out of our power to buy. But what I enjoyed that he did was the interest he took in assisting Brother Joe and myself in the studies that were far too advanced for our years.

Appendix D

Meta Coleman's High Street

Kick the can, good conversations, lightning bugs, homework and good odors from the kitchens filled the evenings on High Street. The weekends held more of the same with the addition of daytime activities—baseball, skating, bicycling and creating equipment for the games. If you didn't have something you tried to make it—carts, basketball nets or tents. You never heard, "You can't play." Every age was accepted. We were all a part of High Street.

There was the mother who pulled all the children's teeth, the one who always made the real lemonade—no imitation mixes were good enough—the one who could make the best hamburgers. Fathers helped with scouting activities and dreamed up ways of getting their offspring to do the yard work. The yard of the mother who made the best lemonade always received the most attention from the High Street gang.

The headquarters for the gang was on the kudzu covered vacant lot which also featured a very tall bag swing hung from a sycamore tree and a small baseball field. Great was the admiration given to one of the mothers who could stand on the top of a slide and jump onto the bag, swinging way out over the kudzu. It was the same mother who made the real lemonade.

None of the mothers worked away from home except one, and she had a kindergarten in her backyard and therefore was always at home. All the neighborhood [children] began their school days in this backyard, and, as a result, this mother was never, even in later years, called by her first name. It was Mrs. because she was the teacher. All the other mothers were on a first-name basis with the children. The kindergarten building was also used for parties and scout meetings.

Backyards were never landscaped except by the children. There were mountains and valleys where the toy soldiers fought, died and were revived. Things were built and dismantled, repainted and painted. Front yards were pretty but not backyards.

Everyone had an assortment of animals—cats and dogs mostly. But the mother with the kindergarten went through rabbits, ducks, guppies and tadpoles for the benefit of the preschool children's education. Every family had an aquarium at one time or another and the children of the mother who pulled all of the teeth had an iron drum filled with water turtles. Almost every family raised a baby squirrel that had fallen out of its nest. The tiny bottles that were used to feed the tiny babies were passed from family to family. It was a sad event in the life of one of the sons of the kindergarten mother when an adult squirrel, raised from a baby, fell into some water in the Kindergarten room and drowned. Dodging bicycles, skates and children, the animals learned to cope with the traffic, and most lived to a ripe old age.

Organized sports are a necessity these days and should be applauded, but there's nothing that can equal the vacant lot ball games. Players were chosen, rules were made and everybody got a chance to play. Arguments sometimes began but were quickly settled by the players. No one bragged about who won. Winning was not that important. Girls could play or watch, and the smaller children were taught by the older children.

Under the blanket of kudzu were tunnels, rooms and all the necessary equipment of a lodge. It is remarkable that no one ever encountered a snake. Wild animals are afraid of noise, and the amount of noise that arose from the kudzu lodge would have frightened anything away.

During the winter months, school, church and scouting activities demanded more attention. But get-togethers still occurred in the playrooms of various families. A doctor is still puzzled as to how one of the children got a fishhook, which was hanging on a wall, imbedded in the top of his foot at that. It's simple. He was jumping on the couch and the fishhook was hanging on the wall. You figure it out.

Yes, there were the usual accidents even though the gang was not far at any time from adult supervision. Falls from bikes, skinned knees, mashed fingers and various broken bones were accepted and healed.

There was one or two in the neighborhood who were a bit more mischievous and who were playing tricks on some of the parents. For instance, a fire cracker in a mailbox. And as soon as some reached the magic age of driving, life in the street for the go-carts, skates and bicycles was not quite as safe.

Halloween was a wonderful time. One father on a parallel street put his heart into the occasion. Just as the trick and treaters arrived at his home, a ghost descended from the upstairs and made eerie sounds as the children scattered. It made Halloween exciting, and the children couldn't wait for nightfall to visit this house.

Easter was a happy time with children endeavoring to increase their knowledge of the Bible and its teachings. Bible study afternoons were held from time to time and the children happily attended if there weren't more exciting things happening. Church activities, however, were attended regularly. Sunday school, church and the Sunday afternoon youth activity were an important part of the week. Being an officer in any religious activity was important. School was also taken seriously, but competition to be the best was not so important. Parents did not compare report cards. Church camps and scout outings were a valuable part of the development of character.

Mothers took children swimming while they shelled peas, talked and admired the progress of swimming and diving skills. Mothers are a wonderful audience. Every now and then an overzealous swimmer was pulled from the water.

Yard service had not developed, and the majority of the yard men were elderly people. The children and yard men enjoyed and respected each other. One young black boy, a friend of one of the yard men, started coming to our neighborhood just to play baseball with the children. He had heard about the children from one of the yard men and became a good friend. He taught them a great deal about the game.

Sources of Information

Almost all the information in this history was gathered in the late 1990s when I was living in Washington, D.C., and where I had access to a host of genealogical and historical sources: the U.S. Archives, the Library of Congress, the DAR library, the National Genealogical Society library, and, of course, a branch of the Mormon Church where I could order microfilm. Over these years I visited all the different state archives and libraries along the southeastern coastline as well as many private and public libraries, particularly in Georgia, such as the Huxford Library in Homerville and the Washington Library in Macon, and so on. Finally, I perused the records in many county courthouses, particularly in Georgia, for deeds, wills, legal records, etc. where most of our ancestors had left bits of information about themselves. As the nineteenth century progressed, local newspapers provided valuable information. Family histories and history books in general were, and still are, even in this internet age, a font of information. Each year there is more available on the internet. As I was putting on the finishing touches of my draft, I subscribed to Ancestry.com to try to try fill in a few gaps. I have listed below some of the genealogical books and histories and listed them by chapter of this book, although, in some cases, a book may have information pertaining to other chapters.

Chapter 1: The Pine Barrens

The Huxford Genealogical Society publishes *Pioneers of Wiregrass Georgia* and *Pioneers of the Wiregrass*, 14 Volumes so far. I wrote profiles of some of our pioneer ancestors that were published in these volumes and which have a little more detail with respect to genealogical information, i.e., dates and names, but are less detailed with respect to their history. You will find profiles of other family members besides the Coleman lineage in the following chapters of this book, so I have not listed this set of books as a resource in them.

Georgia Through Two Centuries, Volume II by Warren Grice (1965). Profile of Daniel Ernest Coleman.

Loose Papers of Tattnall County, Volumes 1 and 2, also published by Huxford, contain scattered information about the four families in this chapter.

Once Upon a Time in Tattnall County, Georgia by Charles Edward Wildes (1990) is a genealogical account of his family which includes a lot of names with dates of the Holland and Coleman families.

Tattnall County Georgia Superior Court Records by Gordon Anthony Thompson (2005).

The Tattnall County Inferior Court Records 1805-1832 by Gordon Anthony Thompson (2003).

A History of Tattnall County: 1801-1865 by John P. Rabun, Jr. (1954).

Tilghman/Tillman Family a genealogical study by Stephen Frederick Tillman (1962) takes one back to this family's origins in England. He edited and revised this book over many years, and it is indispensable for anyone researching this family.

Everett/Everitt Family: A Genealogical History by Alvaretta Kenan Register (1987) is the last word on this family. She is an Everett descendant.

The Descendants of John Crawford of Virginia 1660-1883, no author named. This was written at the behest of Frank Crawford Vanderbilt and provides information about her Everett ancestors as well as her marriage to Commodore Cornelius Vanderbilt.

Sessionville by Patrick Brennan (1996), an excellent account of that Civil War battle.

Treasures of the Longleaf Pines: Naval Stores by Carrol Butler (1998). The best account of the turpentine industry in the southeast U.S.

Chapter 2: Between the Rivers

The Hargrove Family Study by Dorothy Beebe (1993) which gives facts about the origins of our Hargrove line.

Burch, Harrell and Allied Families, Volumes I and II, (Reprinted 1993 and 2005) by Marilu Burch Smallwood provides accounts of the Hargrove, Lee, Hendley and Hamilton families in Dodge County and surrounding counties. Note that Marilu is a Hendley descendant. Also see her *Related Royal Families.*

History of Pulaski County, Georgia by the DAR (1935)

Crisp County, Georgia, Historical Sketches by W. P. Fleming (1932)

The Official History of Laurens County, Georgia, 1807-1941 by Bertha Shepard Hart (1941)

Griswoldville by William Harris Bragg (2000), an excellent account of this Civil War battle

History of Dodge County by Mrs. Wilton Philip Cobb (1932)

Letters from Sister by Wylena Hargrove Davis and Dorothy Hargrove Stoeger (2010) are mostly Davis' letters to various family members about growing up and living in Dodge County in the early 1900s.

Pioneer Days along the Ocmulgee by Fussell M. Chalker (1970) has stories about and names of the early settlers in this area.

The Dodge Land Troubles 1868-1923 by Jane Walker and Chris Trowell (2004) covers the never ending story of the piney woods land disputes around Dodge and Telfair Counties.

The Wests and the Rays and Allied Lines by Nan Overton (1991) provides details on the origins of our Lee lineage.

Chapter 3: Wiregrass Country

History of Lowndes County, Ga. by Mrs. Fred H. Hodges, Sr. (1942)

Shaw Families of the Wiregrass by Harold L. Shaw (undated)

A History of Jones Creek Baptist Church, Long County, Georgia by Elmer Oris Parker (2000). Information on the Horne family.

Our Heritage: A Genealogy of the Descendants of Jacob Carter of South Carolina by Mary Ketus Deen Holland (1974)

Lamb in his Bosom, a novel by Caroline (Pafford) Miller (1933). Pulitzer Prize 1934. Gives a realistic look at the lives of the original settlers in this region of Georgia; by a Pafford descendant and a second cousin of Meta Charles Shaw.

Chapter 4: Florida Territory

The *Reuben Charles Papers* can be perused in the Smathers Library of the University of Florida, Gainesville. See Appendix "B" of this book for more information.

A History of Columbia County, Florida by Edward F. Keuchel (1980)

Echoes of the Past: A History of Suwannee County by the Suwannee County History Committee (2000)

Hamilton County [Tennessee] Pioneers by John Wilson (1998)

Journey into Wilderness by J. R. Motte (1953). An edited journal of a military physician who traveled in Florida during the Second Seminole War. Mentions Charles Ferry and Charles Springs and gives a good account of life and the war in Florida in 1830's as well as Lowndes County, Georgia.

Moses Levy of Florida: Jewish Utopian and Antebellum Reformer by C.S. Monaco (2005)

Ossian Bingley Harte: Florida's Loyalist Reconstruction Governor by Canter Brown, Jr. (1997)

The Territorial Papers of the United States: The Territory of Florida, Volume XXIV (1959)

Spanish Land Grants in Florida, Vol. II by the WPA (1940)

Acts of the Legislative Council of the Territory of Florida by William Wolfe (1991).

INDEX

THE LIGHTWOOD HISTORY COLLECTION

Book 1: *The Lightwood Chronicles: Murder and Greed in the Piney Woods of South Georgia, 1869-1923, being the true story of Brainard Cheney's novel, Lightwood* compiled by Stephen Whigham

Book 2: *Lightwood* by Brainard Cheney

Book 3: *River Rogue* by Brainard Cheney

Book 4: *This is Adam* by Brainard Cheney

Book 5: *Devil's Elbow* by Brainard Cheney

Book 6: *They Don't Make People Like They Used To* by Addie Garrison Briggs

Book 7: *Rivers, Rogues, and Timbermen in the Novels of Brainard Cheney* by Michael Williams, Jr.

Book 8: *When Theo Met Meta: The Coleman-Shaw Families of Valdosta, Georgia: A History* by Daniel Shaw Coleman